Editor-in-Chief and Founder:
    Lyndon H. LaRouche, Jr.
Editorial Board: *Lyndon H. LaRouche, Jr. , Helga
    Zepp-LaRouche, Robert Ingraham, Tony
    Papert, Gerald Rose, Dennis Small, Jeffrey
    Steinberg, William Wertz*
Co-Editors: *Robert Ingraham, Tony Papert*
Managing Editor: *Nancy Spannaus*
Technology: *Marsha Freeman*
Books: *Katherine Notley*
Ebooks: *Richard Burden*
Graphics: *Alan Yue*
Photos: *Stuart Lewis*
Circulation Manager: *Stanley Ezrol*

INTELLIGENCE DIRECTORS
Counterintelligence: *Jeffrey Steinberg, Michele
    Steinberg*
Economics: *John Hoefle, Marcia Merry Baker,
    Paul Gallagher*
History: *Anton Chaitkin*
Ibero-America: *Dennis Small*
Russia and Eastern Europe: *Rachel Douglas*
United States: *Debra Freeman*

INTERNATIONAL BUREAUS
Bogotá: *Miriam Redondo*
Berlin: *Rainer Apel*
Copenhagen: *Tom Gillesberg*
Houston: *Harley Schlanger*
Lima: *Sara Madueño*
Melbourne: *Robert Barwick*
Mexico City: *Gerardo Castilleja Chávez*
New Delhi: *Ramtanu Maitra*
Paris: *Christine Bierre*
Stockholm: *Ulf Sandmark*
United Nations, N.Y.C.: *Leni Rubinstein*
Washington, D.C.: *William Jones*
Wiesbaden: *Göran Haglund*

ON THE WEB
e-mail: eirns@larouchepub.com
www.larouchepub.com
www.executiveintelligencereview.com
www.larouchepub.com/eiw
Webmaster: *John Sigerson*
Assistant Webmaster: *George Hollis*
Editor, Arabic-language edition: *Hussein Askary*

EIR (ISSN 0273-6314) *is published weekly
(50 issues), by EIR News Service, Inc.,
P.O. Box 17390, Washington, D.C. 20041-0390.
(703) 297-8434*

European Headquarters: E.I.R. GmbH, Postfach
Bahnstrasse 9a, D-65205, Wiesbaden, Germany
Tel: 49-611-73650
Homepage: http://www.eir.de
e-mail: info@eir.de
Director: Georg Neudecker

Montreal, Canada: 514-461-1557
eir@eircanada.ca

Denmark: EIR - Danmark, Sankt Knuds Vej 11,
basement left, DK-1903 Frederiksberg, Denmark.
Tel.: +45 35 43 60 40, Fax: +45 35 43 87 57. e-mail:
eirdk@hotmail.com.

Mexico City: EIR, Sor Juana Inés de la Cruz 242-2
Col. Agricultura C.P. 11360
Delegación M. Hidalgo, México D.F.
Tel. (5525) 5318-2301
eirmexico@gmail.com

Copyright: ©2017 EIR News Service. All rights
reserved. Reproduction in whole or in part without
permission strictly prohibited.

Canada Post Publication Sales Agreement
#40683579

Postmaster: Send all address changes to *EIR*, P.O.
Box 17390, Washington, D.C. 20041-0390.

Signed articles in *EIR* represent the views of the authors,
and not necessarily those of the Editorial Board.

A New Era for Human Civilization

EIR Contents

www.larouchepub.com Volume 44, Number 43, October 27, 2017

Cover This Week

Kremlin.ru   Gage Skidmore   Xinhua

A NEW ERA FOR HUMAN CIVILIZATION

The collapse and bailout of the Long Term Capital Management (LCTM) hedge fund, the *wunderkind* of financial derivatives, in September 1998, run by the two 1997 Nobel Prize winners, Robert Merton and Myron Scholes, made it clear to world leaders in Russia, China, and other countries, that LaRouche was right, knew the problem, and more importantly, knew the solution. LaRouche in this article precisely warned "the system simply disintegrates within as short a span as 24 to 72 hours. That is to say, it would vanish as if in a cloud of smoke: in an implosion of what is called 'reversed financial leverage.'" Instead of LaRouche's called-for orderly bankruptcy, the Federal Reserve convened over those 24-72 hours ending on Sept. 23, 1998 with the 16 largest banks on the planet to "solve" the problem by creating the even greater crisis now threatening the lives and livelihood of most Americans. Now is the time for Americans to join in the solution so clearly articulated here.

HELGA ZEPP-LAROUCHE

We Can Enter a New Era for Mankind over the Coming Days

This is an edited transcript of an Oct. 19, 2017 webcast by Helga Zepp-LaRouche.

Harley Schlanger: Hello, I'm Harley Schlanger from the Schiller Institute, and I'd like to welcome you again to our weekly webcast with Helga Zepp-La-Rouche.

There's an absolutely extraordinary event underway in China right now—the 19th Congress of the Communist Party of China. In an address yesterday, President Xi Jinping laid out a bold strategy for the next 35-40 years on how to expand the development of the Belt and Road Initiative (BRI), which has already lifted millions of Chinese out of poverty. This is being treated in the Western media as an opportunity to attack China, to deride the economic model, to talk about how it won't work, even to characterize Xi Jinping as a new Stalin. But while that's the nonsense coming out in the Western media, the Chinese press has been featuring Helga Zepp-LaRouche for her analysis of what's occurring. Today, we have the great benefit of being able to hear directly from Helga. So, Helga, let me turn it over to you.

Helga Zepp-LaRouche: Okay. I recently made a comment to *China Daily*, where I emphasized one aspect of President Xi Jinping's three-and-a-half hour speech, something he mentioned about fourteen times, his emphasis that the aim of politics and of the efforts of the CPC [Communist Party of China], is to create a better and happier life for the people. That is a thought which, when I look at the various politicians in the West—I haven't heard them talking about that. But if you really think about it, that is what politics should be all about. It's no accident that this idea was actually in the American Declaration of Independence: One of the

Feature coverage of Helga Zepp-LaRouche in ChinaDaily. com.cn

inalienable rights mentioned there is "the pursuit of happiness."

I have been in China several times recently, and I have seen that its people are happy; they are optimistic about the future. Look at Xi's speech. He has an incredible perspective which makes total sense, it is realistic, given the fact that China has already lifted 700 million people up out of poverty. If you look at that success story, then you have every reason to believe that the Chinese government will be able to fulfill Xi's vision for the year 2050.

Since this has not been reported very much in the Western media, let me just repeat some of what he said. He said the goal of China is to eliminate all poverty by 2020. In China there are still, I think, 42 million poor people, which is not much, if you remember that China is a country of 1.4 billion. But China wants to uplift all its people so that nobody is left in poverty by 2020. The next goal is that by 2035, China will become a moderately prosperous, modern, functioning socialist country. Then, by the year 2050, China is to become a strong, democratic, civilized, harmonious, and beautiful country, fully modernized. I think this is an incredibly beautiful goal. In his speech, Xi emphasized that, following the century of humiliation for China, which was characterized by the Opium Wars and similar events, China decided not to take any foreign model, but instead develop its own model of "socialism with Chinese characteristics."

Xinhua/Zheng Jiayu

The Three Gorges Dam project in Hubei Province, central China.

I think that the West would be well advised to actually look into what these Chinese characteristics are, because the secret of the success of the Chinese economic miracle, I think, has to be found and can be found in the 5,000 years of Chinese history. President Xi emphasized that in these 5,000 years, China has contributed many things to the development of mankind, and it intends to continue to do so. One of the big contributions of China was not only that Confucius was born and became one of the great teachers of all time, but that Confucianism was actually the state philosophy of China for the better part of 2,500 years, with the short exception of the Cultural Revolution—the ten years from 1966 to '76. Therefore, Confucian thinking and the ideas of Confucius are very deeply ingrained in the Chinese model. I have stated many times that I personally, from studying the speeches of Xi Jinping, have come to the conclusion that Xi himself thinks in Confucian terms.

In his speech, Xi also emphasized that China intends to become an innovation-based society, that the spirit of science must have a very important role. I have seen many times that this is actually what China is doing, by always trying to leapfrog to the newest state-of-the-art technologies. In that way, China has already become a world leader in several categories. All these slanders against China—that it just steals Western patents and Western technologies—may have been the case at the beginning of its "opening up to the West."

By the way, everybody else also takes advantage of foreign technologies. I know of many European business leaders who are convinced that the National Security Agency (NSA) steals. That was just an aside. In any case, China's plan is to become a science-based economy by the year 2025. I think that is very beneficial for all the countries touched by the Belt and Road Initiative (BRI), in the New Silk Road, because China has explicitly offered to share its scientific and technological advances with developing countries. I think this is of great benefit for mankind.

I think this 19th National Congress of the CPC is not just relevant for China. I think the conclusions reached there will radiate throughout the rest of the world, because inevitably everybody looks at this model and asks why is it so successful. Maybe there is something we can learn from it. So we should make sure that everyone really pays attention to the substance of what is going on, and not just to the media accounts which are mostly negative. I always use the example of Hegel, the German philosopher, who wrote in his *Phenomenology of Mind*, that the servant who helps the world-historical individual get dressed, only sees the underwear, and doesn't understand the vision in the mind of the world-historical individual. That's the image I have of the journalists who are writing these ridiculous articles; they are just valets, the servant who helps the great man to get dressed.

Schlanger: It's clear that the Western media is much more interested in underwear than in these physical processes of development. You describe this as a dynamic, global process, and the Western media keeps saying it's going to fail. In particular, they're saying that China is creating a great credit bubble that will collapse. What's the reality there? Why are they wrong, Helga?

Zepp-LaRouche: I think it's ridiculous, because while China has taken credit and has debt, all of this debt is backed up with physical assets. China has this debt because it finances infrastructure projects, industrial parks, hydropower, and all kinds of physical investments—so that, were there a crisis, these physical investments would still be there. They are real, tangible wealth, which is in complete contradiction to the trans-Atlantic financial system's idea of "wealth," which is entirely speculative, and therefore is a complete bubble. It's just funny, because today is the 30th anniversary of Black Monday of 1987. My husband, Lyndon La-Rouche, had forecast the bursting of that bubble at the time, and we have seen a worsening of the situation ever since, because nothing was ever done to correct it. Instead, Alan Greenspan undermined the Glass-Steagall Act, and then finally Larry Summers eliminated Glass-Steagall altogether in 1999. Ever since, there has been incredible deregulation of the financial markets, which then eventually led to the Crash of 2007, which again was forecast by my husband a week before it happened. Finally, the Lehman Brothers-AIG crash of 2008. On this anniversary, many commentators are actually making the point that this crisis, which started in earnest in 2007-2008, is far from over. All the parameters are in fact worse than in 2008; and there are some commentators—even one from the London School of Economics—who say the bullish character of the assets is actually showing characteristics exactly like those

British Guardian *articles warning of a new financial crash.*

before the crash of 1987, and that a big financial explosion could come at any moment in October or November this year.

So, we are all sitting on this powder keg, and it's ridiculous that people are blaming China, the only country which is investing in real goods, for the crash, when these circles themselves are sitting on this powder keg. I think this is something we should urgently address with our campaign to reinstate and implement Glass-Steagall, and our program to return to Hamiltonian economics.

One final word: The attacks on Xi Jinping are coming from people like former *Washington Post* bureau chief in Beijing, John Pomfret, who compared Xi Jinping to Stalin. Such people are just projecting their own evil thoughts onto China; they will not prevail, because they have nothing but words to offer, which mean very little, while China is building a new financial and economic model which brings benefits to all countries that participate. Therefore, China's approach will prevail.

Schlanger: It's clear that the irony here, is that it's a sign of the bankruptcy of Western thinking that we have the biggest bubble in world history in commercial debt, in financial debt, student debt, and car debt—every category of debt is at record levels. Leverage is over the roof. Yet these critics are looking at China, and talking about the China debt. One element of this is that, as you said, it's not just China; there's now a growing interest around the world, because the Chinese have been *doing* something. It's not just something they're talking about doing in the future. Can you just fill us in a little bit on what's happening around the world with the Belt and Road?

The Tide Can Shift Suddenly

Zepp-LaRouche: Most interesting is what's going on in the United States. We are now about two weeks away from President Trump's trip to Asia. He will visit five or six countries, but the most important one will be the state visit to China. I have the feeling that this will lead to some major forms of cooperation between the United States and China—maybe even an official statement that the United States will join the Belt and Road, and work together with China to support the projects of not only the Belt and Road, but also projects in the United States.

The mood in the United States is changing. We had a couple of conferences over the past few weeks, which we either organized ourselves, or conferences we participated in. Many business leaders told us "It doesn't matter what the U.S. government says, because the Belt and Road Initiative is the only way to go. Either we jump on the train of the Belt and Road Initiative, or we will see the lights of the caboose from behind, and we will be left behind." That is exactly the mood which we find in Germany, where, despite the fact that the German government is still stepping on the brake in line with the EU and Brussels, nevertheless, all the other countries of Eastern Europe, of Central Europe, of the Balkans, of Italy, Spain, Portugal, Switzerland, and Austria—they are all moving in the direction of becoming a hub of the New Silk Road. They see its benefits.

The best example, just to give one of many, is what is happening with Greece. Greece was tortured by the Troika—the Internatonal Monetary Fund (IMF), the ECB, and the EU Commission—which imposed the most brutal austerity, characterized by the UN Human Rights Commission as a violation of human rights. Such policies of the Troika have reduced the Greek economy by one-third, shortened life-expectancy, increased the death rate, and led to an incredible emigration of young, skilled labor. This was the policy of the EU. China, on the other hand, now has introduced the Belt and Road policy.

China has built up the Greek port of Piraeus, and is now building a railway northward from the Greek ports

White House

President Trump meeting Greek Prime Minister Alexis Tsipras, Oct. 17, 2017.

to Belgrade and to Budapest—a project opposed by the EU for no good reason. China's initiative has greatly improved the self-confidence of the Greek people. Greek Prime Minister Tsipras was just in Washington, meeting with President Trump. He was accompanied by a large delegation of cabinet members and others. Contrary to the EU, Trump promised reasonable debt relief, real investment in the real economy, and strong cooperation between Greece and the United States. This is a completely different attitude. One outcome is that the United States will be a featured guest at the big trade fair next year in Thessaloniki. These Chinese and American initiatives have increased the self-confidence of the Greek people, who now say that we are no longer at the rim of the EU, but we are now in the center of the Eurasian development.

The spirit of the New Silk Road, which we talked about last time—this is the new thinking that mankind can work together for the common good. It doesn't have to be the case that the geopolitical interests of one group must prevail against the geopolitical interests of another group, but that "win-win" cooperation, where each country benefits, is actually the spirit of this new era. So, this is going on, and I think if you take that together with the developments in Africa and in Ibero-America, this Spirit is marching forward. I am absolutely confident that it will characterize a completely new era of civilization.

Schlanger: You mentioned the Tsipras meeting with

Trump, where Trump spoke about responsible debt relief. This is the second time in a couple of weeks that he's brought up dealing with a debt problem. He talked about doing away with, or cancelling, or writing off Puerto Rico's debt. Now he's talking about the Greek debt needing to be written down, which is obvious except to the bankers who are holding the debt. Obviously this is a big part of the reason, along with his strategic initiative towards China and Russia,

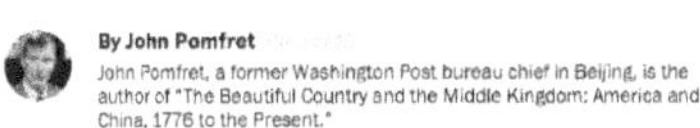

U.S. newspapers demonstrating their anti-Xi Jinping stance.

that there's still a "Russia-gate" attack against him. There are some developments in the last week against that. I wonder if you have some thoughts on it.

Zepp-LaRouche: There is now a very important letter by nineteen Congressmen to the head of the Senate Judiciary Committee, Senator Chuck Grassley, demanding that Special Counsel Robert Mueller be investigated for being biased and having a conflict of interest. I think that is very interesting, and in a certain sense the tide can change very quickly. This was also mentioned by Russian Foreign Minister Lavrov, who at the beginning of the Valdai Forum, which is now taking place in Sochi, Russia, said that the nine months of investigation of the phony Russia-gate story has resulted in absolutely no evidence that there was any collusion of the Trump team with Russia. And he noted very positively, that this has not deterred President Trump from his election promise that he would improve the U.S. relationship with Russia. I think this is very interesting, because, as I have said already in the past—but let me restate it, because it's not self-evident for many people: If the three large countries—the United States, China, and Russia—come to agreement with each other, and stop thinking that it is necessary to have a nuclear build-up and nuclear deterrence and geopolitical maneuvers to outdo one another—we will have the precondition for world peace.

This goes to the whole question of how to deal with the rise of China. Will we believe the line that there is a "Thucydides trap"; will that lead to World War III? Some journalists are retailing that line, saying that is the only future. But I think that if you look at the strate-

gic partnership between Xi Jinping and Putin, and if Trump defeats Russia-gate and continues to seek cooperation with Russia, and at the same time, we see a potential big breakthrough in the context of his state visit to China two weeks from now—then the world will enter a new era, a new stage of development, and the whole world will benefit from it.

For the people of the United States, it's very important not to be caught in the small issues defined by the yellow journalism of the *Washington Post*, the *New York Times* and CNN, who are competing with each other to spread fake news. But you should understand instead, that were the United States and China to work together on the New Silk Road, and if President Trump continues to seek a positive relationship with Russia, then that is in the interest of everybody.

Schlanger: Helga, there's one other area where Americans really have no clue of what's going on, largely due to the media, and that's what's happening in Europe. I refer to the Catalonia separatist vote and the continued flak over that, and the election in Austria where the ruling parties took another big hit, just as they had in Germany. Can you give a sense of what's happening in Europe and how this is part of the same dynamic? Obviously, the Brexit issue is not resolved. So, what's happening in Europe?

Zepp-LaRouche: It is exactly the same dynamic which led to the election victory of President Trump. There are many Europeans who have the feeling that their politicians don't care about their well-being, quite contrary to what Xi Jinping emphasized in his

   A New Era for Human Civilization   7

speech, and contrary to what is practiced in China. For example, look at the present negotiations in Germany to form a so-called Jamaica coalition—Jamaica because the colors of these parties are the same as in the flag of Jamaica; it's the conservative CSU/CDU, the liberals of the FDP, and the Greens. I have not heard any substantial grand design or vision for the future in these discussions; it's all about appointments and minimal agreements. The feeling is that the political class has condoned the fact that the poor become poorer, the middle class becomes more threatened, the rich become richer, and the well-being of everyone is abandoned. Many can't make ends meet. Many feel that the political class has moved entirely away from them. That is reflected in the Brexit, and in the rise of the *Alternative für Deutschland* (AfD), the right populist extremist party in Germany. It's expressed in the right-wing election victory in Austria. And it is expressed in the Catalonia separatist movement, which right now is really moving in a very dangerous direction.

Why is all this happening? The separatists of Catalonia, which is the richest province of Spain, nevertheless feel that they are getting poorer under the present EU regime; and therefore, they want to have a certain independence—a northern autonomy. This is against the Constitution of Spain; the Spanish government of Prime Minister Mariano Rojoy has taken a hard line.

This Catalonia issue is actually a very dangerous development. It's being steered by outside forces. Some Spanish newspapers have accused George Soros of having financed the separatists. Russian media point to a video being circulated by the separatists in Catalonia, which has exactly the same script as a similar video used in the Maidan coup against the Ukrainian government of President Viktor Yanukovych in 2014. It shows women standing in the street, and says that thousands and thousands of people are taking to the streets; then pictures of police violence are shown; then demands that people should support the separatists and spread the word, and so on. Exactly word for word the same video. I would say that the existence of this video points in the direction that it's the same apparatus which was behind the original Maidan, then the "Maidan" against President Trump, and now in Catalonia. What we're dealing with here is really an oligarchical conception. We have long reported that the oligarchy prefers a "Europe of the regions," and not a Europe of strong nation-states that would work together in the tradition of

France's Charles DeGaulle—an alliance of the fatherlands. But destroying the nation-state, and only having regions of perhaps three million inhabitants, would give the oligarchy's supranational structures much greater power, leaving the people without power. So, this is a very dangerous development; it is really the last rearguard battle of the oligarchy.

I think that the other dynamic that I described earlier, the New Silk Road dynamic now becoming stronger in all of Europe, is the one which is advancing more quickly. But it's a turbulent time, and again, I would like all our viewers, listeners, and readers to contact us. The Schiller Institute is providing knowledge about the New Silk Road; we are continuously researching it. We are always putting out more reports about it. We will make more literature available, because you need to know that there is a happy and prosperous alternative to that which the oligarchy has in mind for you.

It is my experience, and I think you, Harley, can confirm it, that once people know about the New Silk Road, they get completely excited. They get optimistic; they say "I have a future. It is worth it for me to study if I'm a young person. I can become a scientist, I can become an astronaut, I can become a teacher. I have a future." That is so important, especially in the United States for example. This terrible opioid epidemic keeps getting worse, and people are full of despair. Or in Europe, where you have many youth in Italy and in Spain who neither have a job, nor are in school. A young person who is neither working or studying, is prone to become either a terrorist, a criminal, violent, or drug addicted, or some other terrible thing. So therefore, the knowledge that there is an alternative strategy whereby we can, together, form a better future is so important. So, please help us to spread the news!

Schlanger: And this is the whole point of these webcasts: To bring to you a picture of the Spirit of the Silk Road, and to give you the capability to ask the right questions and to get the right answers. Again, come to us and engage in a dialogue in an organizing process with us.

Helga, there are going to be a number of events over the next days with China's 19th Party Congress continuing; we'll look forward to hearing from you again on this next week.

Zepp-LaRouche: Okay. Bye-bye.

Party Congress Highlights China's Emergence on the World Stage

by William Jones

Oct. 21—The Congress of the Communist Party of China (CPC), an event held every five years, is the focus of world attention at this critical moment in history. This year saw the election of new party leadership, except for the General Secretary and President of China, Xi Jinping, and Chinese Premier Li Keqiang, both of whom have five more years in their ten-year terms. In the last few years, China has become the engine of the world economy, and the pace of its modernization has been absolutely breath-taking. But this has placed upon China a much larger responsibility that now transcends the mere economic arena, as important as that is—a responsibility of a more general strategic nature.

Xinhua/Lan Hongguang

China President Xi Jinping, delivering a report to the 19th National Congress of the Communist Party of China, Oct. 18, 2017, in the Great Hall of the People.

There were once politicians who claimed that world history is not made below the equator, meaning, in particular, that the course of history is made by the North or more succinctly by the "Western powers," and not by the countries of the "developing" sector. The rise of China has given the lie to this assertion, and has opened the door to a greater say in the direction of the world not only by China, but also by the developing countries generally, with which China has always had a particularly close relationship. Some in the West fear such a development. Imbued with the remnants of Cold War thinking, some Western pundits see any change in power relationships globally as a threat to their interests, and they work to prevent it from occurring.

This geopolitically driven fear has also been obvious in most of the U.S. media coverage of the CPC Congress, where all sorts of grotesque descriptions have been made about the Chinese President and his intentions. One gets the impression that the U.S. media wrote the articles about President Xi's speech at the party congress even before he gave it! They somehow seem to "know" exactly what they want to say, from some template that never really changes, regardless of what was actually uttered. Fortunately, Chinese foreign-language media are rapidly expanding and have not neglected their responsibilities. The flurry of interviews with Helga Zepp-LaRouche in *People's Daily* and *China Daily*, as well as with other friends of China in the West, in connection with the Congress, has helped to break through the information blockade the mainstream media hoped to impose on the general public around this important event. Contrary to the descriptions given in the *New York Times* and *Washington Post*, for example, in the Chinese press there is intense debate over the issues. And Chinese netizens, and their debates and comments, are among the most prolific and argumentative in the world. Unlike their counterparts in the U.S. press, Chinese journalists and netizens are not working off some template.

In his opening speech on Oct. 18, China's President and the Communist Party's General Secretary, Xi Jinping, clearly indicated that the party and the country were now entering a completely new era, and that the CPC would have to take this into consideration as it moves forward towards its celebration of the 100th anniversary of the founding of the People's Republic of China in 1949.

President Xi divided the period ahead into two stages. The first stage will be the period between 2020 and 2035, when China will achieve its full modernization. Then, from 2035 to 2050, China will be transformed into a great modern socialist country that is "prosperous, strong, democratic, culturally advanced, harmonious and beautiful." "In this state we will reach new heights," Xi said. "China's capacity for governance will be achieved. There will be prosperity for all and the Chinese people will be happier and safer. By that time, we will also have become an active member of the community of nations."

Achievements under Xi

In opening the Congress, President Xi outlined the advances made in the last five years, his first term as President. In this period, China capped the achievement of bringing 700 million people out of poverty since about 1980, "with the middle income group expanding." "Arts and culture are thriving," Xi said. "China's soft power and international influence have

Li Keqiang, Premier of the State Council of China.

increased considerably, and there have been advances in the central and western regions. Making development people-centered has paid off. We have been more purposeful in developing green technology, and we have revitalized the armed forces." Xi underlined the efforts China had made in developing major-country diplomacy, pointing as examples of this, to the development of the Belt and Road Initiative (BRI), the creation of the Asia Infrastructure Investment Bank (AIIB), the G-20 Hangzhou meeting and the Asia Pacific Cooperation Forum (APEC) Leaders meeting. "We have made major contributions to global peace and development. The changes have been fundamental and profound. We have solved problems that had never been tackled, and these changes will have far-reaching effects."

A New Era Begins

With the success of these policies, which have been recognized by most of the world, Xi indicated that China was now in a moment of transition. The Congress, he said, was meeting at a time of great importance and in a decisive moment as "socialism with Chinese characteristics" has entered a new stage. "Socialism with Chinese characteristics" is the name given the Chinese model of development since the beginning of the reform and opening up launched by Deng Xiaoping in 1978 after the Cultural Revolution.

In its development over the last 30 years, the ruling Communist Party has played the decisive role. With the end of the Cold War and the collapse of the Soviet Union, the CPC became more intensely focused on improving the livelihood of the Chinese people. While the openness to the West created the preconditions for this growth, it was the leading role of the CPC, Xi said, which provided a direction so that this "openness" would not lead to the type of chaos that had resulted in Russia and other countries that allowed the Western

Deputy Premier Deng Xiaoping, standing next to President Carter in 1979, while on a trip to the U.S.A.

"free market" to run roughshod over them.

One of the goals of President Xi at the present Party Congress was to imbue a renewed commitment to the people's welfare in all the cadre of the Party. "Each Party member must breathe the same breath as the people," Xi said. A major anti-corruption campaign has been ongoing to deal with any Party or government elements involved in corrupt activities. With nearly 90 million members, it's not surprising that corruption has become a problem. While it was young and oppressed, the CPC attracted idealistic people who were ready to put their lives on the line. But as the Party assumed power and its members became powerful and wealthy, many others were allowed to join who were less imbued with high ideals than with a strong desire for a nice career. The new Party leadership greatly reflects the demands that President Xi has placed on the members of the Communist Party with regard to their high moral stature, their whole-hearted commitment to improve the conditions of life of the Chinese people, and their commitment to assume the responsibilities placed on them because of the new role that China must play as a world power.

In his work report, Xi underlined the fact that moving forward with this program would also encoun-

ter obstacles. "It will not be a walk in the park," Xi told the delegates. "We have to address the inadequate and unbalanced development." While economic growth has been the keynote of China's development in the last few years, there are still many people living in poverty and there is a huge gap between the rich and the poor. The contradiction, Xi told the delegates, is between that inadequate development and the people's ever-growing desire for a better life. Xi stressed that it was the Party's commitment to the underlying ideals of socialism, of working for improving the people's livelihood, that was the key to resolving this contradiction. But the commitment to the leading role of the Party was not in question. "We must recognize that this doesn't change our view of socialism with Chinese characteristics. This has not changed, and we must base our work on this reality. China's socialism has entered into a new era of great importance for China and the world."

The Question of Leadership

While outlining the critical importance of the Chinese Communist Party in the last century, as the only instrument then capable of overcoming "feudalism, imperialism and bureaucratic capitalism," Xi made very clear that China was not interested in adopting some foreign model to follow in its social and political development—a point which will no doubt infuriate many self-absorbed Western pundits. "We had to establish a social system that was suited to the Chinese reality and this has created the most profound transformation of the Chinese people. We have reversed the fate of the previous century. Our party has never forgotten its primary mission. We have overcome difficulties and created miracle upon miracle. And today we are closer to, and more confident in, making China's rejuvenation a reality."

As has been characteristic of President Xi's vision since assuming power, there has also been a renewed emphasis on the longer arc of Chinese history and culture, and in his speech, he again placed great stress on the importance of the Chinese people and Chinese cul-

President Xi addresses the Congress.

ture over the last 5,000 years. "In that period, we have made remarkable contributions to mankind. It is the Great Dream of the Chinese people."

And he clearly indicated that the goal of Chinese Rejuvenation, while led by the Communist Party, would be the work of the Chinese people as a whole. Xi underlined the need for developing a socialist democracy, which will entail even greater internal Party debate and discussion over the issues facing the nation and a greater engagement and participation by the other parties in China, which have, since the 1949 founding of the People's Republic, always played an important consultative role in the country's development. These parties as well as non-Party individuals contunue to be welcome to participate in the task of rejuvenation, Xi said.

Changes would also be made in other fields such as strengthening the rule of law, Xi said, a point so often belabored by dishonest Western pundits who have not followed the dramatic developments that have occurred in this field in China during the last years. "We will also develop the broadest and most universal system to protect the rights of the people, and establish law-based governance in all fields. No organization or individual will be able to overstep the law."

And, at the same time, being adequately equipped to play a decisive role on the world stage, China will continue to work to establish that community of shared interest that President Xi has made a hallmark of China's major-country diplomacy. "The world is facing many challenges, and no country can meet these challenges alone nor can it retreat into isolationism. More effort should be made in the call for cooperation in an inclusive world with a shared future. We must stick together through thick and thin."

"Let us seek to learn from one another," Xi continued, in concluding his speech on the work report. "China respects the right of all countries to seek their own path and it will never pursue development at the cost of others. China doesn't threaten any country and we will find a convergence of interests with other countries. We will strengthen cooperation with other developing nations and we will promote cooperation with other nations through the Belt and Road Initiative."

We must hope that the dramatic changes in China will be as infectious here in the United States as they have been in the developing world, where they have sparked new hope in the possibilities of rapid development. We know this paradigm, because once upon a time we also lived it. But we have forgotten the lessons of our own history, and our people have become rather petty and self-absorbed. Only by returning to our roots, to the greatness that we knew under Lincoln or Franklin Roosevelt, can we begin to recover our moral and thereby our industrial strength. If China can lift 700 million people out of poverty in a couple of decades, can we not eliminate poverty in Detroit or Los Angeles or New York? If we can learn to do that, we will see more clearly that China can become our partner rather than our competitor, in developing the world. It is devoutly to be wished that President Xi's message of cooperation and inclusiveness also reverberates with President Trump, so that that lofty goal of a community of common destiny, which President Xi has so often referenced, can at last become a reality. In their upcoming meeting in November, President Trump has an unprecedented opportunity to take the outstretched hand of the Chinese leader and establish a bond that can put mankind permanently on the road to progress. Take his hand, Mr. President!

China's Belt and Road Transforming Southeast Asia

by Mike Billington

Oct. 19—The vast infrastructure projects launched across Asia, Africa, and South America under the impetus of China's Belt and Road Initiative are breathtaking in scope and historically unprecedented. This is certainly the case in Southeast Asia, with new high-speed rail lines, ports and power projects, as well as soft infrastructure such as schools and hospitals, transforming the economies across the region. Xi Jinping announced his plan for a New Silk Road Economic Belt in 2013 in Kazakhstan, for overland development corridors across Eurasia. In the same year, in a speech in the Indonesian Parliament, he announced the 21st Century Maritime Silk Road, to address the island nations and coastal nations of Southeast Asia, South Asia, Africa and the Middle East.

The ten Southeast Asia nations which form the Association of Southeast Asian Nations (ASEAN) are very diverse, with vastly different languages, cultures, religions, standards of living and ethnic makeup. In 2000, following the Asian financial crisis of 1998, ASEAN joined with China, Japan and South Korea, forming the Chiang Mai Initiative to pool currency reserves as mutual protection against any recurrence of the speculate attacks which had devastated the real economies of Thailand, Malaysia, Indonesia and the Philippines in the 1998 so-called "Asian crisis"—which Lyndon LaRouche had then identified as the first ramification of a global financial melt down.

But investments in the desperately needed infrastructure deficit precipitated by the 1998 crisis were at best piecemeal, coming primarily from Japan and South

Chinese President Xi Jinping (center left) and Indonesian President Joko Widodo. Xi announced the 21st Century Maritime Silk Road before the Indonesian Parliament in 2013. Widodo has promoted Indonesia as the Global Maritime Axis.

Korea, with some funding from the Asian Development Bank (ADB) and the World Bank.

By 2014, the ADB estimated infrastructure needs in the region to be at least $800 billion annually, compared to total World Bank lending internationally of $50 billion annually and the ADB of about $10 billion. Thus, when China announced the formation of the Asian Infrastructure Investment Bank (AIIB), only the degenerate Obama administration in Washington (and Japan, tailing after the United States) put up opposition. In addition, China facilitated the New Development Bank established by the five BRICS nations, and set up special funds within China (the New Silk Road Fund and others) intended to spark an infrastructure boom across the region and across the developing sector. Altogether, China intends to invest well more than $1 trillion in the New Silk Road projects.

We present here a survey of the projects across Southeast Asia which are underway or planned for implementation in the near future. It should be noted that the burst in productive activity across the region is also spurring other nations to expand their investments into the booming economic environment, especially since this development of infrastructure lifts the entire productive platform of the region.

High-Speed Rail

Until now, there has been no high-speed rail in all of Southeast Asia. Now, China is building high-speed rail lines in Indonesia, Laos, and Thailand, with projects in the planning stages in several other ASEAN countries. The aim is to connect all of mainland ASEAN via rail, with both north-south and east-west lines, going north to China and west to India and Europe. Eventually there will be bridges to Indonesia as well.

The first approved project was in Indonesia, with a contract to connect Jakarta to Bandung, the third largest city, through a 150 km high-speed rail line. There was fierce competition between China and Japan for the contract, and the bid by the Japanese was better in terms of overall costs. The difference was that Japan, like all investments from the West, demanded government guarantees on the loans, whereas China did not. Indonesia had learned from the massive 1998 speculative attack on its currency by George Soros and his fellow speculators, that providing government guarantees to powers that control international finance can be a death sentence for the economy as a whole. The Indonesian currency was devalued three-fold by speculators: Loans denominated in U.S. dollars, guaranteed by the government in dollars, tripled overnight in terms of their own currency, through no fault of their own. While Indonesia has achieved significant progress since that time, it is still paying the price for those unequal contracts.

China thus won the bid. Construction on the $5.5 billion project began in February 2016, although it has been stalled over land acquisition issues. The Jakarta-Bandung line will cut travel time from three hours to 40 minutes. China Railway Corp's chief engineer said: "This is the first international cooperative project in which China has brought its entire industrial chain

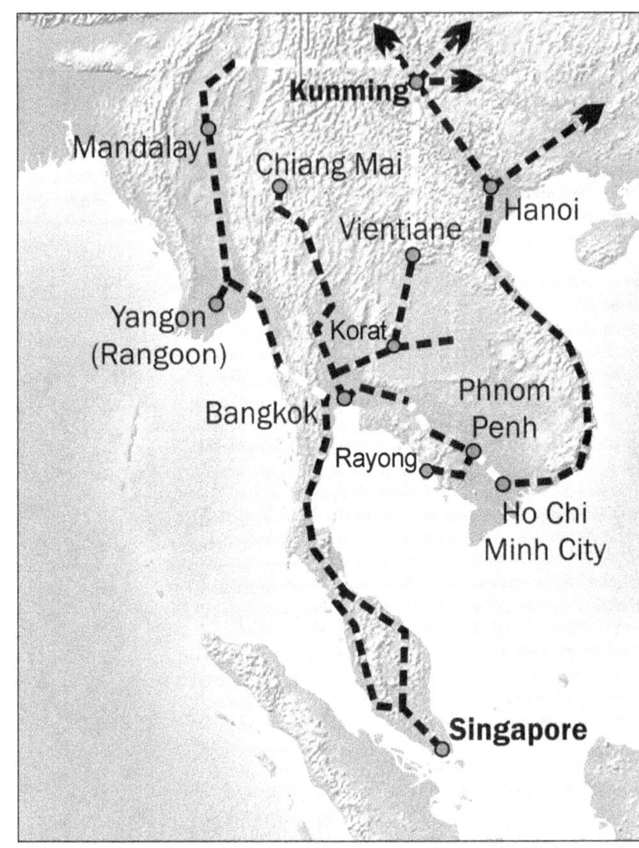

cc/Classical geographer

Long-term proposal for rail network to connect Southeast Asia and China.

model to another country. The complete high-speed railway operation system includes technology, operations, equipment and construction that will be used as a reference for other international projects in the future." The Chinese Ambassador to Indonesia described it as a landmark in the implementation of the Belt and Road Initiative.

The next project to be launched was a north-south line through land-locked Laos. This is the first stage of a high-speed rail connection along the Pan-Asian Highway, from Kunming, through Laos, then to the ports in Thailand, and on to Kuala Lumpur and Singapore. Two branches of this route, in Laos and Thailand, are underway, and a third, in Malaysia, is expected to be launched soon. Japan is also bidding on the Kuala Lumpur to Singapore line.

The Laos line, a 420 km route costing about $6 billion, began construction at the beginning of 2017. An amazing 60% of the route will be bridges and tunnels, with a designed speed of 160 km/h. The project includes the construction of many new roads through the forested rural areas in the north, as well as new power lines—connecting regions that have never had electricity, to the nation's power grid.

There was some concern in Laos about the large number of Chinese workers involved in this rail project, and other Chinese projects in Laos, totaling over 100,000. Laos, however, has only 6.5 million people, with an education system largely oriented to agriculture. While it is true that much of the work on the railroad will be done by Chinese, the many Laotians who will participate will be acquiring skills which will be valuable for future projects. The two governments also agreed that no more than 10% of the unskilled labor, and 20% of the skilled labor, with some exceptions, will be Chinese, and that the permits for Chinese workers will be for two years, or four years at most.

The rail line terminates in Vientiane, near the Thai border, where traditional rail lines connect over the Friendship Bridge to Thailand's Nong Kai and then continue to Bangkok. But this traditional line will eventually be replaced with high-speed rail, both to Bangkok and then to the southeast to connect to the Eastern Economic Corridor ports and industrial zones at Map Ta Phut in Rayong Province, near Cambodia.

The first branch of the Thailand route is beginning construction in October 2017. Prime Minister Prayuth Chan-ocha signed a contract with China while attending the BRICS Summit in Xiamen in September, as one of five invited guests to the Summit. The $5 billion agreement will see a 252 km line constructed from Bangkok to Korat (Nakhon Ratchasima) in the Northeast of Thailand, about half way to the Laos border. Prime Minister Prayuth would like to make Korat the economic hub of the Mekong region, with rail lines extending north through Laos to China, but also east-west connecting to Vietnam, Cambodia and Myanmar. This visionary plan involves integrated water management, upgrading agriculture and industry, upgrading airports and river ports, and tourism. The Northeast (called Isan) is the most populated but poorest region of the country, subject to floods and droughts every year.

Xinhua/Pang Xinglei

Chinese President Xi Jinping and Thai Prime Minister Prayuth Chan-ocha. China is building the first two legs of the Pan-Asian Railroad through Laos and Thailand.

There is a beautiful irony in Prime Minister Prayuth's vision for Korat. The city was once a major hub for the U.S. war on Indochina in the 1960s and 1970s, with a massive U.S. airbase which sent Phantom jets to bomb and napalm Vietnam, Cambodia and Laos, in a war which saw more bombs dropped in that region than all bombs dropped throughout the world in all wars in history. Under this new vision, the city of Korat will instead be the hub for the industrial and agricultural transformation of the region into modern industrial nations. This is the character of the New Silk Road.

The next phase of the Pan Asian Railway, which is expected to be launched relatively soon, is the high-speed rail connection between Kuala Lumpur and Singapore. The plan was agreed to by Malaysia and Singapore in July 2016, with an intention to begin construction in 2017, completing construction in 2026. However, the bidding for the construction is still open, with China, Japan, South Korea, and France all showing interest. China is deeply involved in Malaysian development and is the leading bidder, but it is not certain. China's Ambassador to Malaysia, Dr. Huang Huikang, told *The Star* in July 2017 that China would give the best terms, and would complete the project in five years rather than ten, as proposed by the other bidders.

The 350 km line will be built to have a speed of 300 km/h, running four times per hour, at a cost of $11 billion.

China is now building another rail line in Malaysia, called the East Coast Rail Link. The east coast is far less developed than the west coast, so this line will facilitate a major transformation of the region. The route will connect Port Klang on the Malacca Strait, Malaysia's largest port, through Kuala Lumpur to the east coast, then turn north along the coast to Kota Bharu in Kelantan Province, close to the Thai border.

Prime Minister Najib Razak broke ground for the project in August 2017. The total length of the project is 688 km, with 50 km of tunneling and several underground sections, at an operating speed of 160 km/h and a cost of $13 billion.

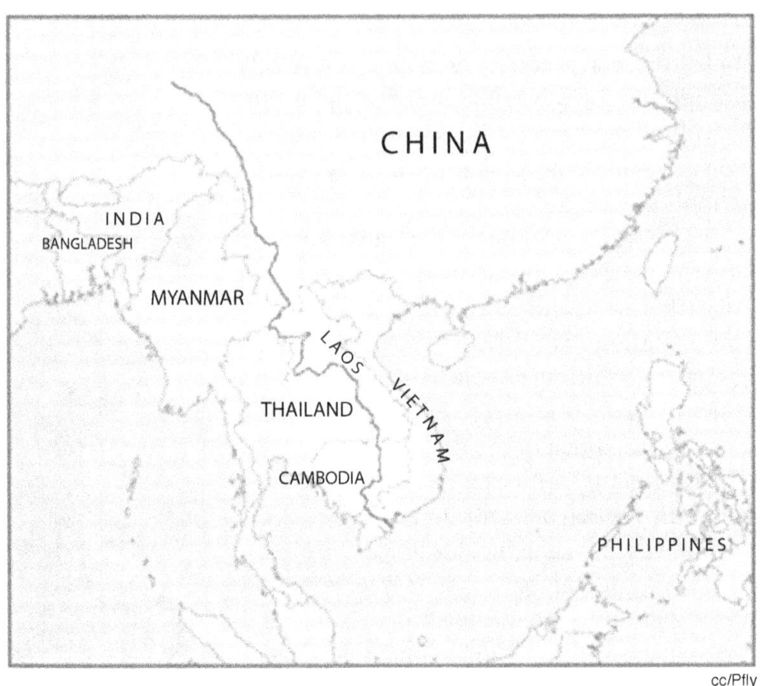

cc/Pfly

The Lancang/Mekong River through China, Myanmar, Laos, Thailand, Cambodia and Vietnam.

Lancang-Mekong Cooperation

Another inter-regional development project under the Belt and Road Initiative is the Lancang-Mekong Cooperation (Lancang is the name of the Chinese portion of the Mekong). The Mekong is the last major river in the world to remain undeveloped, due to colonial divisions and then decades of colonial wars. It was not until 1995 that there was enough agreement among the Mekong nations (Thailand, Vietnam, Cambodia, Laos) that a Mekong River Commission was established. That Commission, however, was heavily influenced by anti-development environmentalist ideology. Earlier efforts to design a model based on FDR's Tennessee Valley Authority (TVA), with hydropower projects, industrialization, and city building, were replaced with conservation measures, efforts to prevent dam construction, and typical IMF/World Bank measures providing minimal help to poor peasants and fishermen while keeping them in a state of backwardness, with no infrastructure development.

A parallel organization launched by the Asian Development Bank (ADB) in 1992, the Greater Mekong Subregion (GMS), bringing in Myanmar and China's Yunnan Province as participants, was far more development oriented. Three main economic corridors were developed, building roads connecting the member nations and providing credit for development along the corridors. Over $18 billion has been invested by the GMS, and nearly double that amount is planned for 107 projects in the pipeline.

With the emergence of the Belt and Road, China has taken measures to expand the vision and the planning for the region. The Lancang-Mekong Cooperation organization was founded in 2015, comprising all six countries along the river. On March 10, 2017, the Chinese secretariat of the Lancang-Mekong Cooperation was opened in Beijing. Foreign Minister Wang Yi said at the ceremony that 45 projects had already been approved and will be completed by the end of 2017, in the areas of connectivity, energy, cross-border economy, water resources and agriculture. Water control is a primary concern, to counter floods and droughts—in March 2016, China opened the floodgates on the Lancang River dams for a period of two weeks, releasing massive amounts of freshwater into the Mekong basin, to help alleviate a drought in Southeast Asia brought on by the El Niño.

China is now carrying out the second phase renovation of the Lancang-Mekong channel, through dredging and rock removal, to facilitate more boat traffic along the river. Plans include building cross-border industrial clusters along the river: China has already developed several industrial parks in the Mekong countries, including the Long Jiang Industrial

China Radio International online

Cambodian Prime Minister Hun Sen attended the September ceremony to open the 400-megawatt Lower Sesan II Hydropower Plant, at Cambodia's biggest hydropower dam.

Park in Viet Nam, Saysettha Comprehensive Development Zone in Laos, Cambodia's Sihanoukville Special Economic Zone and the Thai-Chinese Rayong Industrial Zone. They are establishing agricultural cooperation platforms and programs of poverty reduction across the region.

China is also the leading builder of dams in the world, with the majority of its hydropower projects in Southeast Asia (and many in Africa). The government will start work this year on the $2.3 billion Pak Beng hydropower scheme on the Mekong River in Laos, being built by China's Datong Overseas Investment Company. It is the third of up to 11 dams that Laos is considering for the Mekong. Work has begun on two other large projects being built by the Thais and the Malaysians in Laos. The export of electricity to its neighbors is a major source of income for Laos. Opposition to the dams from Cambodia and Vietnam has been largely mitigated, but the international anti-development NGOs are frantically trying to stop their development.

In Myanmar, a major large scale hydropower project undertaken by China, the Myitsone Dam in the far north of the country, was scheduled to be completed by 2017, and would have been the fifteenth largest hydro project in the world. It was suspended in 2011 due primarily to the instigation of opposition from the regional population, and China has reluctantly concurred, but Chinese companies are nonetheless building other dams around the country, including a 7,100 MW dam in the Shan State, built by China's Three Gorges and Sinohydro, together with Thailand's national power company EGAT. A smaller project is being built in the Karen State by the same partnership. These are both areas of separatist insurgencies over the history of Burma/Myanmar independence from the British, so providing electricity for development will be crucial to the success of the government's efforts to bring peace to the country.

Bilateral Projects— Philippines

The Philippines was largely left behind in the New Silk Road process under the former government of Noynoy Aquino. Following directions from the Obama Administration, Aquino allowed the country to be a pawn in Obama's confrontation with Russia and China, going so far as to

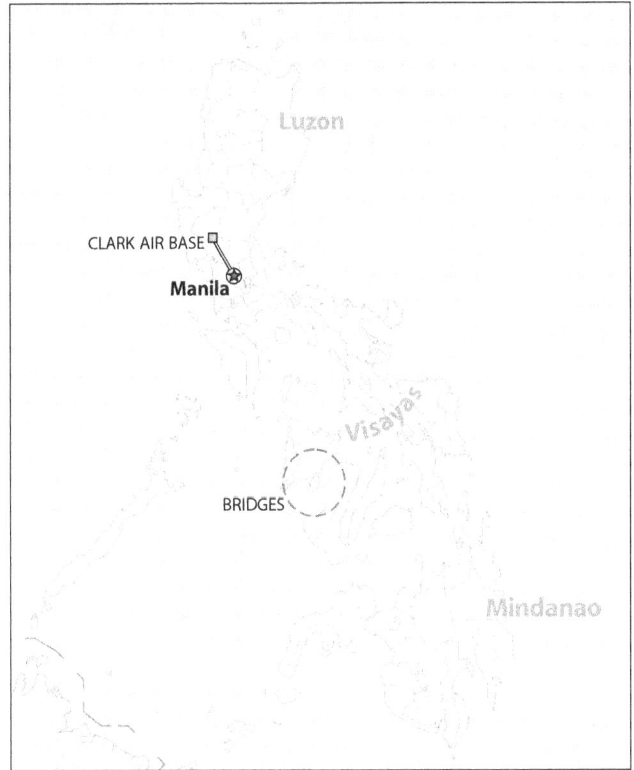

Philippines: High-speed rail connecting Manila with Clark Airbase, and bridges connecting three islands in the Visayas, among the Chinese plans for Philippine development.

A New Era for Human Civilization

file for arbitration under UNCLOS against China over contested sovereignty claims in the South China Sea. Despite winning the toothless arbitration, in which China refused to participate, the victory for Aquino (and Obama) simply encouraged Philippine voters to back the current President Rodrigo Duterte in the following election, in May 2016. Duterte had denounced Obama for trying to provoke a war, and called for cooperation with China's New Silk Road development program—development which was sorely lacking under U.S. tutelage.

Duterte and his Cabinet secretaries immediately began negotiations with both China and Russia on economic and military cooperation. Duterte declared his administration to be "The golden age of Philippine infrastructure," calling his program "Build, Build, Build," with a target of $38 billion to be raised through taxes, foreign and local loans, and official development assistance (ODA) from bilateral partners. China has indicated an intention to provide $9 billion in loans and grants for government-to-government projects, and the possibility of $15.3 billion more in joint ventures and investments by private companies over a six-year period.

In September 2017, a delegation under Finance Secretary Carlos Dominguez visited Beijing, where they arranged a set of infrastructure projects in two phases. The first phase, to be finalized before the ASEAN Summit to be held in Manila in November 2017, includes two major bridges in Manila which are scheduled for construction to begin immediately. Other priorities are a major water control and dam project to supply water to Manila; a Chico River irrigation scheme in the north of Luzon; an elevated expressway in Davao City in Mindanao (Duterte's home town); an industrial park; two drug rehab centers; bridges connecting several islands in the Visayas; an agriculture technical center; and reconstruction of Marawi, the city in Mindanao which was seized by ISIS-linked terrorists in May of this year, and where fighting continued until Oct. 17, when the government forces eliminated the last of the terrorists. The fighting left over 1,000 dead and the displacement of over 300,000.

Many of these proposed projects have been on the books for decades, with promises from the World Bank

cc/Jiur27

The Bataan Nuclear Power Plant in the Philippines—fully completed but never turned on, subverted by the greens and the Washington coup against Ferdinand Marcos in 1986. It can still be restored for operation today.

and others that never materialized. These new projects will likely be funded by the AIIB, China's Exim Bank, or China's Silk Road Fund, perhaps with support from the ADB. The AIIB has also recently agreed to co-finance a flood control project in Manila, together with the World Bank and the government.

The Philippine government has also begun to "test the debt market" in China by issuing yuan-denominated Panda bonds, beginning in November 2017.

With the new momentum in the Philippines, Chinese private sector companies are opening up new investments in the country, both in infrastructure projects and in manufacturing, including aviation, energy, iron and steel, and shipbuilding. China's Huili Investment is planning a $2 billion, world-class integrated steel mill, while Liaoning Bora is launching a joint venture in oil refineries and an oil storage terminal, worth $3 billion. The Duterte government is open to renewing joint oil and gas exploration in the South China Sea, now that both sides have returned to the earlier policy of Deng Xiaoping, that sovereignty issues should be put aside while the two nations cooperate in joint development.

The Chinese investment has also spurred Japanese business to show increased interest in both infrastructure and industrial investment in the Philippines.

Although no agreements have been reached as yet, there is intense discussion with China on two major rail projects in the Philippines. The first is a high-speed

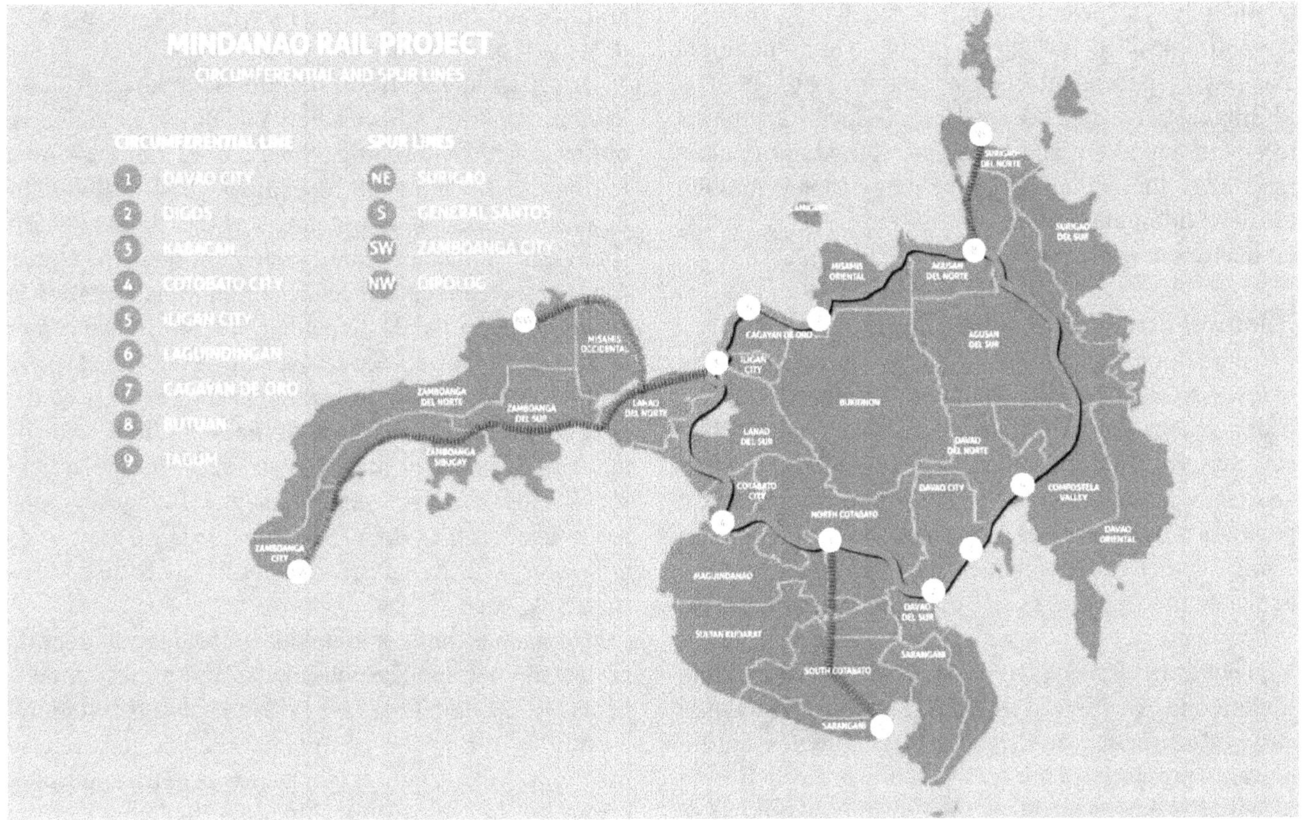

Skyscrapercity Davao Region Facebook

Ring Rail plan for Mindanao in the Southern Philippines.

rail connection between Manila and the Clark Airbase, formerly a U.S. military facility, now an international airport. China had been contracted to rebuild that rail line in 2003, but the contract was terminated by the Aquino Administration in 2012 under pressure from Obama.

Clark Airbase is only 58 miles from Manila, so a high-speed rail connection would make it a viable alternative international airport for the capital city, whose only international airport is horribly overcrowded.

Also, Chinese Vice Premier Wang Yang led a forty person delegation to a forum in March 2017 on a proposed Mindanao railway, an 830 kilometer project estimated to cost $4.2 billion, creating a ring rail and connecting the major cities of the largest, and poorest, Philippine island. Wang said China would conduct a feasibility study on the project.

Lyndon LaRouche has always considered the Philippines to be the critical nation in Asia in bridging the divisions of East and West, having a tradition in both Eastern and Western cultures. He has long promoted the ring rail and the industrialization of Mindanao as a central issue in unleashing the Philippines' potential for development.

Mindanao has been the site of independence movements from factions of the Muslim (Moro) community, as well as terrorist movements instigated by Saudi backed Wahhabis connected to al Qaeda and ISIS. China's intention under the Belt and Road is not to avoid areas of instability, but rather to consider such conditions to be a motivation to invest, as a means of achieving peace through development. Other port and airport development projects in Mindanao are also under consideration.

Most important, the future of the Bataan nuclear plant is under discussion with China, Russia and others. The nuclear plant stands unused as a symbol of the regime change carried out against nationalist President Ferdinand Marcos in 1986 by George Shultz and the emerging neoconservative movement in the United States. The nuclear plant, the first in Southeast Asia, was fully completed and ready to turn on, when foreign-funded green NGOs repeatedly stalled the project, until the Washington-orchestrated coup shut it down

   A New Era for Human Civilization   19

completely. The next government nonetheless paid for the entire project, leaving the nation energy deficient and paying exorbitant energy rates up to today. The Philippine LaRouche Society has led a lonely campaign to restore the plant, and to use small modular nuclear reactors to furnish energy to the many islands making up the Philippines. Now, finally, the issue is on the table. Here too, China can play a leading role.

Bilateral projects—Indonesia

In addition to the high-speed rail China is building to connect Jakarta and Bandung, referenced above, China is engaged in infrastructure development projects across the huge Indonesian archipelago of over 18,000 islands, which are home to the fourth largest population in the world. A former head of the Indonesian Chamber of Commerce told a Washington, D.C. audience in 2016 that nearly every infrastructure construction project in the country had a Chinese name.

The former President of Indonesia, Susilo Bambang Yudhoyono, who served from 2004 to 2014, hosted two large infrastructure conferences in Washington during his term, presenting a master list of projects which were essentially shovel-ready, if foreign funding and construction capacity could be arranged. He estimated the country needed about $450 billion per year in infrastructure funds to restore the nation's economy. He came up essentially empty handed on both trips. The United States has invested in mining and oil exploration, but for any infrastructure, it demanded government guarantees, of the sort that had killed Indonesia when the speculators drove its currency down in 1998. As reported above, this is what killed the Japanese bid for the Jakarta-Bandung rail contract. It is to Yudhoyono's credit that he refused to accept the unequal terms, but in the process, he ended up with virtually no new infrastructure.

The U.S. share of foreign direct investment (FDI) in Indonesia has collapsed from 8.3% in 2013 to under 2% in 2016, despite Obama's pledge of greater support to Asia, and especially to Indonesia, where he spent part of his childhood.

Xi Jinping's 2013 announcement in Indonesia of the 21st Century Maritime Silk Road recalls the historic Chinese Treasure Ships of the 14th and 15th century. The world's largest ships of that time, and the largest armadas, sailed to Indonesia as part of their exploration, which also took them to India, Africa,

and through the Red Sea to Egypt, and perhaps even to Italy, it has recently been learned.

In 2014 the current Indonesian President Joko Widodo "Jokowi" was elected, and quickly arranged a meeting with Xi Jinping. Speaking at the East Asia Summit in Myanmar in November 2014, Jokowi announced his vision of Indonesia as the "Global Maritime Axis" of the new paradigm emerging in the world. "Indonesia realizes that a substantial transformation is taking place in the 21st century," he said. "The center of gravity of the geo-economic and geo-political world is shifting from West to East. Asian countries are on the rise. As the world's largest archipelagic state with its strategic location at the cross roads of the Indian and the Pacific Oceans," Jokowi said, "Indonesia must assert itself as the Global Maritime Axis." Clearly, this coincides with Xi's vision of the 21st Century Maritime Silk Road.

China has built a number of bridges and ports across the nation. The Suramadu Bridge, which connects Surabaya in East Java with the island of Madura, spanning 5.4 km, was completed in 2009, long before the New Silk Road. It is the longest trans-oceanic bridge in Southeast Asia. Since the launching of the Maritime Silk Road, China has rapidly expanded investment, increasing it five-fold over the span of 2016, becoming the second biggest investor after Singapore by the beginning of 2017, including investment in over 1,200 industrial, mining and infrastructure projects. Indonesia's Investment Coordinating Board chief, Thomas Lembong, said that "China's rate of investment growth means it is only a matter of time before it takes over first place." Projects under discussion include integrated infrastructure development in North Sumatra, and a new harbor and nuclear industry construction in North Kalimantan.

ASEAN-China

To detail the extensive transformation of the Southeast Asian economies under the Belt and Road Initiative is beyond the purpose of this report. A few general points of conclusion will suffice.

China has become the leading trade partner of all ten of the ASEAN nations, by a wide margin in most. Even the wealthy states of Singapore and Brunei are rapidly expanding their economic cooperation with China. In Brunei (the fifth wealthiest nation in the world), China is building a $3.5 billion oil refinery, while China Telecom is expanding the Sultanate's cell phone networks, and a Chinese electric car factory is being constructed.

Singapore, which for several years now has been the largest foreign investor in China, is now also the largest Chinese investment destination in Asia, and Singapore's largest trading partner.

China has built new ports across the region. In Myanmar, China is building a deep sea port in Kyauk Pyu in western Rakhine state, near the Bangladesh border, which is the terminus of the oil and gas pipeline constructed through Myanmar to Kunming, completed in 2015. Both the port and a connected industrial zone will transform the region economically. In Malaysia, one of the leading recipients of Chinese Belt and Road investments, a new port facility, called Malacca Gateway, is being built south of Klang, the current port on the Malacca Strait. A new bridge to Penang from the Malay mainland is under construction by the Chinese. A Chinese industrial zone with over 100 industries is in operation at Cambodia's only deep water port at Sihanoukville, while over 30 Chinese agricultural and agro-industry projects are in place in Cambodia, including rubber and rice facilities. Northern Laos is now supporting extensive banana production facilities built by the Chinese.

In Thailand, the historic effort to build a canal across the Kra Isthmus in southern Thailand, connecting the Pacific and the Indian Oceans, has recently been given new life due to China's Belt and Road Initiative. Friends of the LaRouche movement in Thailand, who have fought for this great project for over 30 years, have recently won support from leading figures in the Thai military, the Privy Council, and business layers, who joined together in a forum in Bangkok on September 11, 2017, with representatives from China, Japan and others to encourage the government to adopt the program, with support from China's Belt and Road institutions as well as Japan's Global Infrastructure Fund.

In Vietnam, which has had political and military

Xinhua

The Cat Linh-Ha Dong urban railway project in Hanoi, Vietnam, seen on March 28, 2017, is being constructed by China Railway Engineering Corporation.

conflicts with China over centuries, China is nonetheless the largest foreign investor, with over $56 billion in nearly 5,000 projects, mostly in manufacturing.

The new middle class in China is also the source of nearly half the tourism in the region, which is a significant source of income in the beautiful Southeast Asian countries.

The picture is clear. The U.S. effort, heightened under the Obama Administration, to divide Asia along the old Cold War lines—either support the United States or support China—has collapsed. Obama's attempt to isolate China economically with the Trans-Pacific Partnership (TTP) was already failing, but has been finished off by President Trump. The ASEAN proposal for a Regional Comprehensive Economic Partnership (RCEP), based on fair trade and equality among all the Asian nations, has been fully supported by China and is now close to implementation.

Geopolitics, based on the idea that one nation can gain only at the expense of others, is being dumped into the garbage pail of British imperial ideology, as Xi Jinping's win-win approach to achieve a common destiny based on shared interests is bringing the world together for the common good. As President Trump prepares to visit Asia and meet with Xi Jinping in November 2017, it is to be wished that the result will see the United States fully join the New Silk Road process, marking a dramatic step towards the end of empire forever.

British Monarchy Escalates Attack on The New Paradigm in South Africa

Oct. 23—British Lord Peter Hain is leading a new, escalated attack on the South African flank of the New World Paradigm of the BRICS and the Belt and Road Initiative (BRI). His fake news is that South African President Jacob Zuma and members of his family are part of a criminal "transnational money-laundering network"; in announcing this in the House of Lords on Oct. 19, he signalled the British Crown's orchestrated offensive against President Zuma and his faction in the ruling African National Congress (ANC)—including Nkosazana Dlamini-Zuma, his preferred successor as ANC President and President of South Africa.

CC/Number 10

The despicable attempt at regime change in South Africa starts here. Here, the old bag reads her speech to the House of Lords in 2007, accompanied by her consort, Prince Lizard.

R.P. Tsokolibane, leader of LaRouche South Africa, released a statement today on this new attack, reprinted below, drawing attention to the implications for the BRICS.

Hain served under Tony Blair—of Iraq War ill-repute—variously as Minister for Africa, Minister for Europe, Leader of the House of Commons, Privy Counsellor, and Lord Privy Seal. The Queen raised him to a life peerage in 2015.

Hain wrote to Chancellor of the Exchequer Phillip Hammond on Sept. 25, expressing his concern that two banks, HSBC and Standard Chartered, may have "wittingly or unwittingly" laundered funds for what he calls the "Gupta/Zuma criminal network," a "transnational money-laundering network." His letter names more than forty members of the Zuma and Gupta families, some other individuals, and related entities. The list includes the names of President Jacob Zuma and Nkosazana Dlamini-Zuma.

Hammond responded "with a straight face," as one might say, reporting, with all possible gravity, that he has referred Hain's letter to British law enforcement agencies, including the Serious Fraud Office. The U.S. Department of Justice and FBI have also been brought in.

This fraudulent attack comes just two months before the ANC election of a new party president, who will become the party's candidate for President of South Africa in 2019. The chief contenders for party president are Dlamini-Zuma and London's candidate, Cyril Ramaphosa, who scarcely conceals his satisfaction over the British attack on the Zuma faction. Ramaphosa said on Oct. 20 that the South African state has been "captured by people who want to milk the state, who want to rob our country of the money that belongs to the people," and called on public servants to testify "when a commission of inquiry into state capture is set up." (That "narrative" includes the now familiar condemnation of any major infrastructure investment by the government as "looting.") South Africa's opposition parties have also opportunistically chimed in, in support of the British attack.

At an overflow campaign rally for Dlamini-Zuma in Evaton Township not far from Johannesburg, Oct. 22, attended by LaRouche South Africa leader R.P. Tsokolibane, members of her team were aggressive in denouncing the British attack. Earlier in the day, Dlamini-Zuma's aide, Carl Niehaus, told the press, "We are not going to be told, by British people who think they can still behave like colonialists and [can continue] neocolonial behavior, how we should deal with a situation in our country!"

Tshepo Kgadima, political analyst for South Africa's African News Network television (ANN7), commented that evening, that Hain "wants to ensure that colonial rule will reign supreme on the peoples of this land, and that is despicable." It is "nothing but the return of the old enemy that has been there from the time that we established democratic rule in South Africa." Indeed it is, and a look at history shows that the old enemy has been active in South Africa for a much, much longer time.

Tsokolibane's statement follows.

—David Cherry

British Relaunch Old Scandals To Try To Stop Our Move to the New Paradigm

by Ramasimong Phillip Tsokolibane

Oct. 23—I have watched, with some amusement, the open and direct efforts of the British Empire to relaunch some old fake scandals against our President and his family, in the form of an investigation by the British Treasury. While President Jacob Zuma's ex-wife, Nkosazana Dlamini-Zuma, who is a candidate to succeed him, has strongly denied the charges of money laundering made by a member of the British House of Lords, Lord Peter Hain of Neath (or is it of the "Underneath"?), I would not have dignified such charges with a denial. This is fake news made by a former South African, with long-standing connections to the "anti-corruption" campaigns run and funded by organizations linked to George Soros, the British asset and former Nazi speculator. I am informed that the accuser was himself accused of corruption over his conduct in a Labour Party election campaign; the Crown's prosecutor, to whom the London Metropolitan Police had referred the case, simply declined to prosecute.

As expected, the same networks and British assets in South Africa that have long been screaming for the head of our President, have echoed this "Lord Ha-Ha" and are demanding a similar investigation in South Africa, lest we be embarrassed by the British probe. But as authorities here were quick to point out, such investigations have been ongoing, and, I must assert, they have found nothing thus far worth prosecuting.

What I know is that the British Empire hates our President, because he has had the audacity to align South Africa with the emerging new economic paradigm coming from the East, under the principal direction of President Xi Jinping's China and President Vladimir

GCIS/Sbusisiwe Magwaza

Dr. Nkosazana Dlamini-Zuma is the candidate of the ruling ANC's Zuma faction to succeed President Jacob Zuma. Here, she dances with the Department of Home Affairs' choir at a Presidential Banquet in 2012 to bid her farewell, upon her election as Chairperson of the African Union Commission.

Putin's Russia, both in the creation of the BRICS alliance (of Brazil, Russia, India, China, and South Africa) and China's Belt and Road Initiative (BRI) for vast and rapid economic development. President Zuma and South Africa will assume the rotating chairmanship of the BRICS early next year. This is what London fears, and it is what the corrupt British legal system is desperate to derail— through its puppet Lord Hain.

These specious charges are not new; they have been floating around British-linked press sewers and other outlets for some time. Lord Hain, with coordination from the City of London, now seeks to give them a patina of validity by having the Brits themselves conduct the investigation against President Zuma, his family, and his allies—the strange and mysterious

Dlamini-Zuma was Minister of Health under Nelson Mandela, of Foreign Affairs under Presidents Mbeki and Motlanthe, and of Home Affairs under President Zuma, before assuming the African Union's highest office.

Gupta interests. The timing of Lord Hain's action is also intended to provoke maximum chaos in the processes within the African National Congress, which will select, in December, a successor candidate to President Zuma, who supports his ex-wife.

While many South Africans have a propensity to believe that their government is massively corrupt, and that individuals such as the Gupta brothers have bought influence, I suggest that the greatest corruption of our political life comes from the same British Empire sources that Lord Ha-Ha represents, who want us to toe the Empire's geopolitical and economic line, instead of acting in our national interest in aligning with the BRICS and the BRI. If our President merely wished to enjoy only riches and celebrity, the easiest path for him would be to sell out our interests to the British, as many of our political figures have already done.

Instead of issuing a denial of the self-righteous Lord Ha-Ha's accusations, I say the British Empire has no authority to pass judgment on these matters! Instead, charge London with blatant interference in the sovereign political affairs of South Africa, in much the same way that the British, through 'ex' MI6 agent Christopher Steele interfered in the U.S. election and is continuing to interfere in political affairs of the United States, by creating the "Russia-gate" hoax against President Donald Trump. The political movement of former U.S. Presidential candidate and economist Lyndon La-Rouche, of which I am the leader in South Africa, has

taken the point in exposing this fake news hoax directed by Wall Street operator and amoral legal assassin Robert Mueller.

President Trump has recently zeroed in on British agent Steele's fake dossier on him, and is demanding to know who was behind it. One would hope that President Zuma would take a page from the feisty American President, and demand an investigation of who this "Lord of the Under-Neath" is really working for, and how the British government has directly involved itself in this fraudulent hoax here.

More importantly, we should drive our British Empire enemies even more crazy with anger, by our President declaring that South Africa's movement into the new paradigm of peace and prosperity as represented by the BRICS and the BRI is irreversible and will continue, regardless of what happens to him or his successor, because it represents the true will and destiny of our people. And, we should increase the tempo of nuclear and other development projects which are part of this process.

The Brits, in their desperation to undo what will not be undone, have exposed themselves as the true authors of the efforts to destabilize my country, albeit with the assistance of their assets in the United States, linked to the despicable Soros, and inside the administration of their asset Barack Obama, the anti-African former President. This should provide the spur to our President to initiate actions that cause us to finally exit the British Empire and its so-called Commonwealth, as I have been calling for, for some time. Why remain in a hornet's nest that has already stung us, and worse, more than once?

And, just to drive the Brits even more insane, I propose that President Zuma issue a formal invitation to another of their "hateds," President Trump, to visit South Africa so that he might see for himself both the problems created by British Empire/City of London forced underdevelopment, but also the potential for the development of our nation into a fully modern agro-industrial giant, capable of leading Africa into a new era of growth and prosperity. By the year 2050, more than four out of ten of all the globe's people will reside in Africa.

Never respond to the British or any enemy on their terms, created by fake news and lies. Tell people the truth behind what is happening, and let them laugh at these pathetic little tricks. Oh, how the British hate that! As Mr. LaRouche always says, "have fun," because if you are having fun, rest assured, your enemies are not.

ramasimongt@hotmail.com

Hail Columbia, Happy Land!

by Robert Ingraham

A CONTRIBUTION TO
AN ONGOING DISCUSSION
Part II of Two Parts

Part I was published in EIR, *Oct. 20, 2017.*

V. The Revolution Betrayed

Oct. 13—The Society for the Colonization of Free People of Color of America (American Colonization Society) was founded on Dec. 21, 1816, only one year after the conclusion of the disastrous War of 1812. Henry Clay presided over the founding meeting, and later served as president of the Society from 1836 to 1849. Other founding members included (president-elect) James Monroe, Andrew Jackson, Francis Scott Key, John Randolph, and Richard Bland Lee. James Madison served as its president in the 1830s and Thomas Jefferson was an avid supporter. These men were all slave-owners.

The Society was formed for one reason only: to preserve and strengthen slavery in the United States. Some of its supporters may have been taken in by phony humanitarian rhetoric, but the intention, as stated openly by its leaders, was to secure and spread the slave system.

In his opening speech to the ACS convention, Henry Clay declared, "Can there be a nobler cause than that which ... proposes to rid our country of *a useless and pernicious, if not dangerous portion of its population?*"

Henry Clay

The plan, as envisioned by the Society, was not to send black Americans back to Africa, but to deport only *free blacks*, i.e., American citizens. The slaves would all be kept in America. By sending free blacks to Africa, two related aims would be served. On the one hand, the free blacks in the North who wanted full citizenship and voting rights could be gotten rid of. At the same time the problem of having free blacks living side by side with slaves in the South could be solved. It may come as a surprise to some, but between 1776 and 1861 there were always more free blacks in the South than in the North, even after the northern states had emancipated their slaves. Having these free men and women living in the same communities, and intermingling with slaves in Virginia, Georgia. and South Carolina, was very dangerous for the slave owners. A slave would look at a free black and ask the obvious question: "Why am I not free"? The ACS wanted to eliminate the free blacks, and thus more easily control the slaves—to enforce total subservience. A foretaste of this had already been seen in 1806 when Virginia enacted a law forcing all newly manumitted slaves to leave the state within a year or be re-enslaved.

Support for the Society was widespread among some of the most powerful figures and political leaders in the nation, Democrat and Whig alike. In 1819, the ACS received $100,000 from Congress,[1] and on Feb. 6,

---

1. That same year, Henry Clay would cast the tie-breaking decisive vote forcing slavery on the newly organized Arkansas territory, the first time

Arthur Tappan

Rev. Joshua Leavitt

Lewis Tappan

1820, the first ship, the *Elizabeth*, sailed from New York for West Africa with three white ACS agents and 88 black "emigrants" aboard.[2] Not only Congress, but individual states funded the ACS. In 1829, the Pennsylvania Assembly endorsed the American Colonization Society and agreed that black removal would be "highly auspicious to the best interests of our country," and as late as 1850, Virginia set aside $30,000 annually to fund the ACS.

The Moral Decline of the Nation

For sixty consecutive years, with the brief interlude of the four-year Quincy Adams Presidency, America was led by Presidents who either advocated or acquiesced to the enslavement or subjugation of human beings. This included the twenty-four year domination of the Virginians Jefferson, Madison, and Monroe, as well as the twelve years of Jackson and Van Buren. Not surprisingly, those five Presidents were also the most hostile to Hamilton's economic thinking and to his vision, as to the future and purpose of the American Republic.

Some might argue that the creation of the Second National Bank or the imposition of high tariffs sig-

naled a return to the principles of 1776 and 1787, but is this really the case? Is such an argument morally sound? Will your conscience allow it? Fundamentally—and emphatically—the paradigmatic issue in America has always been about the People, or more precisely, about the true nature of Man. This was the driving, passionate issue of the Revolution. This is what Hamilton understood. With the election of Jefferson in 1800, the nation began to lose its way; the mission that had been defined by the Declaration of Independence and the Constitution weakened and ebbed. From 1801 forward, the acceptance and promotion of slavery doomed the nation, precisely because it was a *profound betrayal* of the Revolution itself. Gouverneur Morris understood this.

A case could be made that many of the supporters of the ACS were otherwise decent people. Some were what we would call today "canal builders," individuals who supported economic development and other worthy causes. But the hard core of the ACS were all racists, and they agreed with Thomas Jefferson that blacks were an intellectually inferior sub-species. The truth is that after the murder of Hamilton, and during the twenty-four year uninterrupted rule by slave owners from 1801 to 1825, the nation's commitment to the intention of the Revolution was nearly annihilated. There were good people who did good things,

---

slavery had been officially allowed in the greater Louisiana Territory.

2. The year of Clay's "Missouri Compromise," which gave official national recognition to slavery.

but a fatal moral disease had been injected into the nation's culture.

The Assault

Beginning in 1801, the previously-anticipated full citizenship rights for emancipated blacks in the North were delayed or halted, and in some cases existing rights were rolled back. In the South, voluntary manumissions were outlawed in most states, slave codes were strengthened, and slavery was spread—first into the deep South, then the Louisiana Territory, and ultimately into Texas. Physical attacks against abolitionists became common; some abolitionists were murdered outright. Attacks like the one on Brown's New York Theater, were repeated against many targets throughout the North.

In 1834, a series of anti-abolition riots, lasting four days, took place in New York City. This began when Arthur Tappan, a white abolitionist, attended a religious service and sat in a pew next to the black Samuel Cornish. James Watson Webb,[3] the publisher of the *Courier and Enquirer*, printed lurid scare stories of impending inter-racial marriages, black ministers with white mistresses, and other filth to fan the flames. The home of Lewis Tappan, who in 1839 would help organize the *Amistad* defense, was destroyed and burned to the ground. The home of Reverend Joshua Leavitt, editor of *The Evangelist* and a manager of the American Anti-Slavery Society, was attacked. The home of Reverend Peter Williams, Jr. was attacked, and the St. Philip's Episcopal Church was demolished. All told, the mob targeted the homes, businesses, churches, and other buildings associated with the abolitionists, particularly black religious leaders.

Cassius Marcellus Clay

In the decades leading up to the Civil War, these scenes were repeated in city after city throughout the North and Mid-West including in Boston, Philadelphia, and St. Louis. One of the worst riots took place in Cincinnati, Ohio. One black abolitionist, Elijah P. Lovejoy of Altoons, Illinois, who published a religious journal *Observer*, was shot and killed in November 1837, as he emerged from a building that a white mob had set on fire.

By 1836, the ACS had succeeded in even prohibiting the mere discussion of slavery on the floor of Congress with the infamous Gag Rule.[4]

This all led into the horrors and near death of the American Republic in the 1850s, with the passage of Henry Clay's Fugitive Slave Law, the expansion of slavery into the territories, the Kansas-Nebraska Act, and the Dred Scott decision. The hour of destiny was fast approaching for America.

Clay versus Clay

As a young man, Henry Clay was tutored by George Wythe, a signer of the Declaration of Independence. Wythe, a Virginia planter, freed all of his slaves, because he found slave-owning to be incompatible with that Declaration to which he and the other signers had pledged "our Lives, our Fortunes and our sacred Honor." Perhaps due to a lasting influence from Wythe's earlier instructions, at a 1799 convention to revise the state constitution of Kentucky, Clay put forward a proposal for the gradual abolition of slavery in Kentucky, and at that time he gave several anti-slavery speeches. Clay's 1799 proposal was defeated, and he never again raised the issue of emancipation for the remainder of his life. Instead, the adult Clay bought a 600-acre plan-

---

3. Webb was a New York leader of the American Colonization Society. Earlier, he had been a supporter of Andrew Jackson, but by the 1830s he had become a close friend and ally of Henry Clay. In fact, Webb claimed to have coined the name for their new party, the Whigs, in a column he wrote in the *Courier and Enquirer*.

4. Here again, it was John Quincy Adams, as in the *Amistad* case, who rose to defend freedom and Constitutional government. Bear in mind, however, that the Gag Rule was imposed against the anti-slavery petition campaign, organized primarily by black abolitionist leaders.

tation, owned 60 slaves, and engaged in the buying and selling of human beings until his death.

Contrast the downward progression of Henry Clay, with the dynamic which governed the life of his second cousin, Cassius Marcellus Clay. Cassius Clay, nicknamed the "Lion of White Hall," was the son of one of the wealthiest planters and slaveholders in Kentucky. Initially, he was a plantation owner, and a member of the Kentucky elite. However, after attending several abolitionist meetings in Boston, he began to question the morality of his chosen path. He freed all his slaves and began to speak out against slavery. An influential member of the Kentucky House of Representatives, he lost re-election, and his political career was destroyed.

During a political debate over slavery in 1843, Cassius Clay survived an assassination attempt. Despite being shot in the chest, he drew his knife and cut out the eyes of his assailant. Again, in 1849, while making a speech supporting abolition, Clay was attacked by six men, who beat, stabbed and tried to shoot him. Clay fought off all of them, using his knife to kill the leader.

In 1845, Clay began publishing an anti-slavery newspaper, the *True American*, in Lexington, Kentucky. Within a month he received death threats. Shortly thereafter, a mob of sixty men broke into his office and destroyed his printing equipment. Clay then moved his newspaper to Cincinnati, Ohio, and continued to publish.

Clay became one of the founding members of the Republican Party, and in 1861 Abraham Lincoln appointed Clay as Minister to Russia. In St. Petersburg, Clay secured Russian support for the Union during the Civil War, which led to the deployment of the Russian fleet to New York and San Francisco to protect those harbors against the British navy.

In 1862, when Lincoln appointed Cassius Clay a major general with the Union Army, Clay publicly refused to accept the appointment unless Lincoln would agree to emancipate the slaves under Confederate control. Clay was then deployed by Lincoln to assess the mood for emancipation in the border states in the months preceding the Emancipation Proclamation.

Every individual makes choices, and those choices determine specific paths, specific trajectories. The choices made by the cousins Clay are very instructive. The one led step-by-inevitable step to the near destruction of the nation; the other, beset by sacrifice,

violence and political banishment, led to the glorious victory of 1865.

VI. The Revolution Affirmed

By the late 1830s, the white abolitionists William Lloyd Garrison and Wendell Phillips began to argue for the dismemberment of the United States. By so doing, the two of them, together with their followers, became pawns in a British Empire plot to destroy this nation. Beginning with their Act of Abolition in 1834, the British, incredibly, began to put themselves forward as the premier anti-slavery nation in the world—a stunning gymnastic feat, since the British Empire had been the controller of the world slave traffic for the previous 150 years, and had been responsible for the deaths of millions of Africans. The British, who also controlled the purse-strings of the slave-owning South due to their hegemony in global cotton trade, backed the Garrisonites and egged on both sides—creating what modern sociologists call a "gang/counter-gang" dynamic, intended to split and ruin the United States.

Garrison's argument was that America, its Constitution, and all of its political institutions had been racist and pro-slavery from the start, and that the only way to purify the nation was to secede from the slave-owning states and to form a new nation free of America's pro-slavery origins. Garrison condemned both electoral activity and other political initiatives as a futile effort to save a nation that did not deserve to be saved.

The most damning and influential rebuttal to Garrison's argument came in 1845 with the publication of a pamphlet titled *The Unconstitutionality of Slavery*, authored by a man named Lysander Spooner. More will be said about Spooner later, but it is important to note that—although Spooner's pamphlet had great influence—he was not the first to lead the charge against Garrison's treasonous schemes.

Between 1833 and 1840, the American Anti-Slavery Society, led by Garrison and based in Boston, was the leading abolitionist organization in the country. In 1840, angered by Garrison's attacks on the Constitution, almost all of the black leaders of the Anti-Slavery Society split off, and together with white allies, founded the New York-based American and Foreign Anti-Slavery Society. The split was led by Samuel Cornish, Theodore S. Wright, Samuel Ringgold Ward, Charles B. Ray, and Amos Beman, and they were joined by white allies, including Arthur and Lewis Tappan, William Jay (John Jay's son), and Gerrit Smith.

Many of these individuals went one step further, founding the Liberty Party as a new political party. In 1844, the Liberty Party's presidential candidate James Birney received 62,103 votes (2.3%) nationwide, but almost 17,000 of those votes came from New York, which cost Henry Clay the electoral votes of New York and thus the Presidency. The Liberty Party platform of 1844 declared that it would treat the fugitive slave clause of the U.S. Constitution "as utterly null and void, and consequently forming no part of the Constitution of the United States," on grounds of "natural right" (natural law). It also contained a plank demanding "the absolute and unqualified divorce of the general government from slavery...."

During the brief decade of its existence, it was the leadership of the Liberty Party who insisted, who demanded, that America must honor the principles of the Declaration of Independence and the Constitution. They refused to abandon the battle. In 1854, many Liberty Party members played important roles in the founding of the Republican Party.

Interlude—a Shifting Battlefield

In looking at these developments, which evolved over a 20 to 30 year time-span, one must abandon the academic armchair and recognize the ongoing degeneration of the nation during those years, and the courage displayed in the face of murderous opposition by those who defended America's revolutionary heritage. By the 1840s and 50s this seemed an impossible challenge.

There was a great moral erosion among many of the white abolitionists. Some went over to Garrison and his pleas for dis-unity. An even larger number succumbed to the American Colonization Society. The American Convention for Promoting the Abolition of Slavery, the national convention of anti-slavery societies, stopped opposing colonization in 1821 and openly endorsed it

Gerrit Smith

in 1828. By 1829, many of the leaders of the New York Manumission Society were backing colonization.[5]

Among black leaders, a parallel change is also apparent. By 1840, the giddy days of 1808, when thousands paraded in the streets to celebrate the end of the African slave trade and the dawn of a new era, were long gone. Decades of broken promises and oppression had taken their toll. If one looks at the writings, sermons, and speeches of black abolitionists, from say 1775 to 1855, a great change is observable, beginning after 1815/1820, but then becoming very pronounced by 1840. The change in character is essentially one of a people betrayed. Anger and desperation begin to be heard. This is seen as early as 1829 in David Walker's "Appeal To the Coloured Citizens of the World." It is also seen in the writings and speeches of Theodore S. Wright and Henry Highland Garnet, both of whom, by the late 1840s, began calling for armed slave uprisings.

By the 1850s, seeing no way out, a number of black leaders, such as Garnet and Abraham Shadd, even began to support emigration, although the preferred destinations were Canada or the Carribean, not Africa.

The general desperation was further fueled by the failed slave uprisings—and the brutal revenge which followed them—of 1800, 1811, 1822, and 1831. It is easy—looking back almost two hundred years—to academically dismiss these uprisings, but consider the words of Gabriel, the leader of the 1800 revolt. After being caught, tried, and condemned to death, Gabriel made a final statement before he was hanged, in which he said, "I have nothing more to offer than what General Washington would have had to offer, had he been

---

5. While many white leaders waffled on colonization, it was the black abolitionists who took the lead, rejected colonization, and demanded full citizenship rights. Indicative is a declaration by a black woman named Maria Stewart, who in a speech in Boston rejecting colonization, stated that before she would be driven back to Africa, "the bayonet shall pierce me through."

taken by the British and put on trial. I have adventured my life in endeavoring to obtain the liberty of my countrymen."

Yet, the fight was never abandoned. The overwhelming majority of the people involved in running the Underground Railroad were black. The same is true for the Vigilance Committees, the organizations which protected runaway slaves and fought the Fugitive Slave Law. Many of the people involved were, themselves, former slaves.

Harriet Beecher Stowe

Levi Coffin

Essentially, by the 1850s, many northern blacks and their white allies were engaged in what only can be called classic guerilla warfare against the slavocracy.

The White Abolitionists

It is important to mention here a handful among the white abolitionists. There is great courage to be found among their ranks. The Tappan brothers played a key role in recruiting John Quincy Adams into the *Amistad* defense. Gerrit Smith was the great ally of Frederick Douglass. Others, not mentioned here, were important participants in the Underground Railroad and other activities. Admittedly, mistakes were made by some of these people. Yet, whatever errors of judgement occurred, they were made under conditions of constant warfare; the moral intention was always steadfast:

Arthur and Lewis Tappan: In 1833 Arthur Tappan was a cofounder of the American Anti-Slavery Society, serving as its first president. He split with Garrison in 1840 to found the American and Foreign Anti-Slavery Society. In New York he was perhaps the most steadfast white ally of Samuel Cornish, Charles Ray and other black leaders. His home was targeted during the 1834 anti-abolition riots. After the Fugitive Slave Law of 1850 was passed, Tappan refused to comply with the new law and donated money to the Underground Railroad. Arthur's brother Lewis Tappan played a paramount role in the *Amistad* case, and in recruiting former President John Quincy Adams to represent the kidnapped Africans. In 1846, Lewis founded the American Missionary Association, which built more than 100 anti-slavery Congregational churches. After the Civil War, Lewis founded numerous schools and colleges to aid in the education of freedmen.

Gerrit Smith: a wealthy New Yorker, Smith was, without question, the leading funder of the Underground Railroad, the Liberty Party, and resistance to the Fugitive Slave Law. Smith was the Liberty Party candidate for President in 1848. He was also a friend of Lysander Spooner, and he became one of the leading advocates of the view that the United States Constitution is an anti-slavery document. He was instrumental in winning his friend Frederick Douglass to that view. In 1852, he was elected to Congress from the Free Soil Party, but he resigned his seat in protest of the passage of the Kansas-Nebraska Act.

Levi Coffin: Coffin was a Quaker, as were many of the early abolitionists. He became one of the most prominent leaders of the Underground Railroad, leading more than 3,000 fugitive slaves to freedom. He was given the name of "President of the Underground Railroad" by his contemporaries, and reports he conveyed to Harriet Beecher Stowe became the basis for *Uncle Tom's Cabin*.

Rev. Joshua Leavitt: a Congregationalist minister, Leavitt became a prominent writer, editor and publisher of abolitionist literature. He was also a spokesman for the Liberty Party. In 1841, Leavitt published his "Financial Power of Slavery," in which he argued that the slave system of the South was destroying the economy of the nation.

The Beecher Family: Henry Ward Beecher was the first pastor of Congregationalist Plymouth Church in Brooklyn. His church became an important Underground Railroad station, through which slaves from the South were secretly transported to Canada. Beecher's sister was Harriet Beecher Stowe, author of *Uncle Tom's Cabin.* Abraham Lincoln's Cooper Union Address is today famous, but what many people don't know is that it was Beecher, in October, 1859, who invited Lincoln to New York and offered him $200 to speak at the Plymouth Church. Lincoln accepted the invitation, traveled to Brooklyn and participated in church service on Sunday, Feb. 26, 1860. When it became apparent that the church was not large enough to hold the anticipated audience, the venue for Lincoln's address was changed to the Cooper Union, where he spoke before a capacity crowd of 1,500 the following day.

Lysander Spooner

Human Slavery Is Unconstitutional

In 1845, Lysander Spooner published *The Unconstitutionality of Slavery,* a work that would come to have a powerful impact on the Liberty Party, Frederick Douglass, and ultimately on Douglass' relationship with Abraham Lincoln. Spooner was a rather erratic personality. His career is punctuated by several initiatives of a somewhat dubious nature. Yet, there is no arguing with the powerful effect unleashed by the publication of his work on slavery.

The text of *The Unconstitutionality of Slavery* pursues three parallel themes. First, an exhaustively researched and documented record of the United States in regard to the legality of slavery, including an examination of the constitutions and laws of the pre-revolutionary colonies, the Articles of Confederation, the post-revolutionary state constitutions, and the U.S. Constitution.

In the course of presenting his evidence, Spooner demonstrates that at no time was slavery actually legal in pre or post-Revolution America. This may seem, to today's Americans, an incredible statement, but Spooner is very meticulous in his research. None of the charters or constitutions in the pre or post-Revolution colonies and states, including in the South, actually contained wording which legalized slavery; none of them even defined slavery, or who was subject to being enslaved; none of them contained wording restricting slavery to individuals with black skin. Spooner demonstrates that slavery was an "accepted social practice," but never a legal institution. It was simply imposed on the colonies—with no legal basis—by the policies of the British Empire.

Spooner's second subject is a scrupulous examination of the text of the U.S. Constitution, and the proceedings of the 1787 Constitutional Convention. He takes the Constitution apart, clause by clause, and shows that nowhere is there to be found a legal endorsement or establishment of slavery—that slavery was never constitutional as a national institution. On the contrary, the wording of the Constitution itself is specifically and clearly anti-slavery in its content. Some, today, might howl at this analysis, pointing to the three-fifths clause and the fugitive slave provision, but Spooner deals with all of this in the course of his examination. His arguments are far too lengthy to reproduce here, but his pamphlet is now in the public domain and readily available to those who wish to read it.[6]

Spooner's final and most powerful theme is that slavery is unconstitutional because it violates Natural Law. He argues that slavery is contrary to the nature of Man and contrary to the recognition of that nature in the Declaration of Independence, the founding document of the United States. Spooner's argument is that the American Revolution was fought on behalf of this Natural Law conception, to which slavery is profoundly contradictory. The Declaration of Independence created the new nation based on this understanding of the human identity; thus, all subsequent laws enacted by states are invalid if they contradict it. He says:

The people of this country—in the very instru-

---

6. https://www.amazon.com/Unconstitutionality-Slavery-Lysander-Spooner/dp/1508601704

ment by which they first announced their independent political existence, and first asserted their right to establish governments of their own—declared that the natural and inalienable right of all men to life, liberty and the pursuit of happiness, was a "self-evident truth."

VII. Douglass and Lincoln

In this section, the words of Frederick Douglass will do most of the speaking. The facts of Douglass' life are well known and readily available. The only subject that will be documented here is that his commitment to human freedom and human development, as it was set forward in the principles of the American Revolution, was uncompromising. Initially, Douglass distrusted Abraham Lincoln and didn't particularly like him. A large part of this antipathy stemmed from Lincoln's long-standing association with the American Colonization Society, an organization which Lincoln never actively participated in, but one whose goals he had praised on many occasions.

Eventually, the two men became very close. Their bond transcended the realm of practical politics and specific issues. One of the things which is striking is the willingness of both men to abandon previously held positions if they found them to be faulty, and to then act decisively, based on the implications of their newly-discovered insights. During their first meeting, when Douglass accused Lincoln of vacillating on the issue of slavery, Lincoln responded that although he "might seem slow to make a decision, I think it cannot be shown that when I have once taken a position, I have ever retreated from it."

Douglass broke sharply with William Lloyd Garrison on the nature of the American Republic. When Garrison publicly burned copies of the Constitution as a racist document, Douglass severed all relations with him. Douglass read and studied Spooner's *The Unconstitutionality of Slavery* and became a vocal proponent of its findings. He became a major leader in the Liberty Party, working with Gerrit Smith. On July 5, 1852, Douglass delivered a speech to the Rochester Anti-Slavery Sewing Society. This speech is now famous and is usually given the title "What to the Slave is the 4th of July?" Unfortunately, many current versions of that speech are presented in an abridged or edited form, one which emphasizes Douglass' attacks on racism but leaves out the heart of his argument. We present here excerpts which are often omitted:

I differ from those who charge this baseness on the framers of the Constitution of the United States. It is a slander upon their memory, at least, so I believe. There is not time now to argue the constitutional question at length; nor have I the ability to discuss it as it ought to be discussed. The subject has been handled with masterly power by Lysander Spooner, Esq., by William Goodell, by Samuel E . Sewall, Esq., and last, though not least, by Gerritt Smith, Esq. These gentlemen have, as I think, fully and clearly vindicated the Constitution from any design to support slavery for an hour.

Fellow-citizens! there is no matter in respect to which, the people of the North have allowed themselves to be so ruinously imposed upon, as that of the pro-slavery character of the Constitution. In that instrument I hold there is neither warrant, license, nor sanction of the hateful thing; but interpreted, as it ought, ought to be interpreted, the Constitution is a *Glorious Liberty Document*. Read its preamble, consider its purposes. Is slavery among them? Is it at the gateway? or is it in the temple? it is neither. While I

Frederick Douglass

do not intend to argue this question on the present occasion, let me ask, if it be not somewhat singular that, if the Constitution were intended to be, by its framers and adopters, a slaveholding instrument, why neither slavery, slaveholding, nor slave can anywhere be found in it. What would be thought of an instrument, drawn up, legally drawn up, for the purpose of entitling the city of Rochester to a track of land, in which no mention of land was made?....

Now, take the Constitution according to its plain reading, and I defy the presentation of a single pro-slavery clause in it. On the other hand it will be found to contain principles and purposes, entirely hostile to the existence of slavery....

Abraham Lincoln delivering his address at the dedication of of the National Cemetery at Gettysburg, Nov. 19, 1863

I, therefore, leave off where I began, with hope. While drawing encouragement from the "Declaration of Independence," the great principles it contains, and the genius of American Institutions, my spirit is also cheered by the obvious tendencies of the age.... change has now come over the affairs of mankind.

In the same speech, after reading from the Declaration of Independence, Douglass says:

From the round top of your ship of state, dark and threatening clouds may be seen. Heavy billows, like mountains in the distance, disclose to the leeward huge forms of flinty rocks! That bolt drawn, that chain, broken, and all is lost. *Cling to this day—cling to it,* and to its principles, with the grasp of a storm-tossed mariner to a spar at midnight....

Abraham Lincoln

Abraham Lincoln concluded his Gettysburg Address with the words:

....from these honored dead we take increased devotion to that cause for which they gave the last full measure of devotion—that we here highly resolve that these dead shall not have died in vain—that this nation, under God, shall have a new birth of freedom—and that government of the people, by the people, for the people, shall not perish from the earth.

What was that "new birth of freedom"? Was it not a return to the freedom declared in 1776 and 1787? Was it not a reaffirmation of the principles embedded in the American Republic from the beginning?

In Abraham Lincoln we see the same unity of purpose which existed in Hamilton. The economic policies, the nation-building, the adoption of Public Credit. For Lincoln, as for Hamilton, these are all inseparable from the cause of human freedom and development. It is the sacred conception of Man, and the moral commitment to the uplifting of the people which defines the future. Lincoln's victory put an end to the sixty-year desecration of the nation. It was—in every sense imaginable—a new birth of freedom.

Lincoln always hated slavery. Unlike Henry Clay, he found it horrifying and morally abhorrent. For many years, however, under Clay's influence, he saw no domestic solution, and he supported colonization, even as late as 1862. His greatness is that he broke with that view—and he broke with it not simply for pragmatic political reasons, but because he reached a moment where it was no longer compatible with his moral intention—just as Douglass had broken with Garrison.

The Emancipation Proclamation, issued in September 1862 and taking effect the next January, was the defining act of Lincoln's immortality, the action which made possible that "new birth of freedom." Lincoln's proclamation contained no mention of compensation for owners, made no reference to colonization; the emancipation was immediate, not gradual. Lincoln addressed blacks directly, not as property subject to the will of others, but as free men and women, citizens of the Republic. This was the Second American Revolution.

A month after Lincoln issued the Emancipation Proclamation, Frederick Douglass sent a message to Lincoln:

> We are all liberated by this proclamation. Everybody is liberated. The white man is liberated, the black man is liberated, the brave men now fighting the battles of their country against rebels and traitors are now liberated.... I congratulate you upon this amazing change—the amazing approximation toward the sacred truth of human liberty.

And in 1876, in his "Freedmen's Monument" speech, Douglass recalled:

> Can any colored man, or any white man friendly to the freedom of all men, ever forget the night which followed the first day of January 1863, when the world was to see if Abraham Lincoln would prove to be as good as his word? I shall never forget that memorable night, when in a distant city I waited and watched at a public meeting, with three thousand others not less anxious than myself, for the word of deliverance which we have heard read today. Nor shall I ever forget the outburst of joy and thanksgiving that rent the air when the lightning brought to us the emancipation proclamation.

VIII. Martin Luther King

In looking at the lives of those Americans who kept lit the beacon of freedom in the early Nineteenth Century, one must take note that many among the most important leaders were ministers. Richard Allen, Samuel Cornish, Absalom Jones, Charles Bennett Ray, Peter Williams, Jr., James Varick, Lewis Woodson, Theodore S. Wright, and others were all deeply religious men. These were not men who had a practical agenda; neither did they view their lives'-work as the single issue of "black equality."

And they certainly had nothing in common with the infantile shallow "multi-culturalism" and "identity politics" we see too much of today.

As was reborn in the adult personality of Martin Luther King, these individuals saw their mission as one of developing a human society—to uplift humanity from backwardness, illiteracy, ignorance, and brutishness; to develop a culture and

Martin Luther King, Jr.

institutions coherent with the creative potential within each individual human soul, to make possible opportunities for each new child to experience the beauty of growth, happiness, and development. This all flowed from the promise of the American Revolution. In his Aug. 28, 1963 "I Have a Dream" speech in Washington, D.C., Martin Luther King said:

> Five score years ago, a great American, in whose symbolic shadow we stand today, signed the Emancipation Proclamation. This momentous decree came as a great beacon light of hope to millions of Negro slaves who had been seared in the flames of withering injustice. It came as a

joyous daybreak to end the long night of their captivity.

In a sense we've come to our nation's capital to cash a check. When the architects of our republic wrote the magnificent words of the Constitution and the Declaration of Independence, they were signing a promissory note to which every American was to fall heir. This note was a promise that all men, yes, black men as well as white men, would be guaranteed the "unalienable Rights" of "Life, Liberty and the pursuit of Happiness." It is obvious today that America has defaulted on this promissory note, insofar as her citizens of color are concerned. Instead of honoring this sacred obligation, America has given the Negro people a bad check, a check which has come back marked "insufficient funds."

But we refuse to believe that the bank of justice is bankrupt....

I have a dream that one day this nation will rise up and live out the true meaning of its creed: "We hold these truths to be self-evident, that all men are created equal."

Martin Luther King remains to this day the best of America. People who never met him sensed in him a deep love for what America could and should become. And they responded to it. On Jan. 16, 1995, at an event in Washington, D.C., honoring Martin Luther King on King's birthday, Lyndon LaRouche had the following to say:

I want to bring Dr. Rev. Martin Luther King back to life, in the sense that there is a part of him I probably know better than many people who were close to him while he walked the Earth. I never had the chance to speak to him, never even the chance to shake his hand, though I lived through the same events through which he lived. And yet, I know him in some ways better than most of the people who were close to him, because I know his development. I know a transformation from a dedicated young preacher coming out of Atlanta going to Boston, coming out of Boston University, going from there to take up a parish, then being elevated by a happenstance, almost, to assume a position of leadership, and going

through succession of crisis after succession of crisis....

In making the last public address of his life, in reflecting upon the cup of Gethsemane, he walked to the podium, before thousands of people, and said, "I am drinking the cup. I wish to live, but I am drinking the cup." And he laid forth a mission.

The difference between Martin and many other people who might envy his position, is that they don't understand one thing: that they would have had to give up something in themselves, a reluctance in themselves, to make each of those successive steps by which he stepped upward. Faced with a challenge from which many people would pragmatically have retreated, he moved ahead. He found the next higher level of action to carry out. And he not only decided to carry it out, because many of his associates also decided to carry out the action with him; but what he decided, was to present the conception of the action to the people in ways that the people would grasp the idea....

The civil rights movement was not a creation of the late 1950s and 1960s. The civil rights movement has existed as long as there was slavery in the United States. There was always somebody fighting for the same thing; and the level of fight against slavery in the middle of the Nineteenth Century, was on a higher intellectual level in many respects, than was the fight for civil rights in the Twentieth Century....

The moment of truth is approaching, and when we look at Martin, we remember him not only for his ideas, but we remember him for that which made him a leader, and we try to find in ourselves the equivalent quality.

When you are faced with a challenge, with the threat of defeat, do you, like Sancho Panza, go practical on us, and do you concern yourself only with your own personal position; or do you bring that within you, that creative power which is the distinguishing power of man in the image of God, and do you apply it to the problem that we face, to participate in developing the ideas which, given circulation, can give a movement the identity it requires to do the job which it is destined to do, and must do?

Can you find in yourself some of that quality of Martin? Can you develop and purify yourself, to find in yourself, something of that quality of Martin, rather than Sancho Panza? If you can, if enough can, then we can win. And the time has come to win. And the time for preparation is growing very short.

IX. Our Rebirth

Racism exists in America today. Everyone knows this is true. But from whence did that racism arise? It was not born in America. It is not part of the genetic make-up of white Americans. Racism, and the practice of slavery, are a heritage derived from Empire and Oligarchism. Find its roots in ancient Rome. Find it in medieval Venice. Find it in the Dutch and British Empires of the Seventeenth and Eighteenth Centuries. Oligarchical dominion, human bondage, the pursuit of monetary wealth and power—this is all the heritage of oligarchical rule. This is the horrifying nightmare which colonists traveled to America to escape.

The American Revolution was a declaration of war against that old oligarchical system; and that revolution has been the light of the world for the last two hundred and forty-one years. Nor was the promise of that revolution limited to eradication of chattel slavery. Remember Franklin Roosevelt's dedication to the plight of the Forgotten Man. The promise of America is intended for all of the people.

Look at the misery in our nation today: the poverty, the drugs, the homelessness, the suicides. The discarding of whole sections of the People—throwing them on the scrap-heap to be ignored and forgotten: This is tearing out the soul of America. That is our great moral crisis.

Martin Luther King's 1963 Washington, D.C. speech was spoken fifty-four years ago, the same year as the murder of John F. Kennedy. During all of these subsequent years, we have been living through a dark and utterly demoralizing time. Is it not time—is the date not already past due—for our own "new birth of freedom"? The patriots of the Nineteenth Century lived through sixty years of betrayal from 1801 to 1861. Is it not now our time to cash the promissory note, to achieve justice for all Americans, for all of our people together?

Our enemy resides in the oligarchical elite of London, Wall Street, and Brussels. They seek to divide us, to pit us against each other. They know that the people are desperate, and desperate people, people who are losing hope, can be infused with rage, manipulated and defeated. The rich are getting richer, and the poor are getting poorer. How better to maintain power than to have the poor fight among themselves?

The solution to this crisis will be found in the mind, the morality, and the mission of Alexander Hamilton, the organizer and founder of the United States Constitution. Remember the American Revolution. As Frederick Douglass said of the Declaration of Independence, *"Cling to this day—cling to it,* and to its principles, with the grasp of a storm-tossed mariner to a spar at midnight."

Bibliography

Allen, Richard, *Eulogy for Washington* (*Philadelphia Gazette,* 1799).

Douglass, Frederick, *Fourth of July Oration* (July 5, 1852).

Dubois, W.E.B., **The Negro** (New York: Holt, 1915).

Foner, Philip & Branham, Robert James, editors, **Lift Every Voice—African American Oratory 1787-1900** (Tuscaloosa, Alabama, University of Alabama Press, 1998).

Harris, Leslie M., **In the Shadow of Slavery—African Americans in New York City 1626-1863** (Chicago: University of Chicago Press, 2003).

McAllister, Marvin, **White People Do Not Know How to Behave at Entertainments Designed for Ladies & Gentlemen of Colour** (Chapel Hill: University of North Carolina Press, 2003).

Quarles, Benjamin, **Black Abolitionists** (New York: Oxford University Press, 1969).

Sidney, Joseph, *An Oration Commemorative of the Abolition of the Slave Trade in the United States* (New York City: 1809).

Spooner, Lysander, *The Unconstitutionality of Slavery* (Boston: Bela Marsh, 1846).

Wheatley, Phillis, *Poems on Various Subjects, Religious and Moral* (London: A. Bell, 1773).

White, Shane, **Stories of Freedom in Black New York** (Cambridge, Massachusetts: Harvard University Press, 2002).

Williams Jr., Peter, *An Oration on the Abolition of the Slave Trade* (1808), and *Slavery and Colonization* (New York: July 4, 1830).

A TALE OF TWO PARADIGMS

Why the West Must Join China's Belt and Road Initiative

by Harley Schlanger

Oct. 20—The 19th Congress of the Chinese Communist Party opened on Oct. 18 with a powerfully optimistic speech by President Xi Jinping, in which he presented a bold strategy for the continued advance of China's economy, as a contribution toward realizing "the common destiny for mankind and enduring peace and stability." President Xi outlined how China would build on its extraordinary progress in reducing poverty, saying that by 2020, poverty in China will be completely eliminated, and by 2035, the nation will be fully modernized. While the driver for this is the extension of the New Silk Road into a global landbridge, centered on the Belt and Road Initiative (BRI), Xi spoke of the thinking behind it, which includes promoting the "spirit of science" and classical culture, to make China an "innovation society."

The Schiller Institute's Helga Zepp-LaRouche, an early advocate and promoter of the New Silk Road, has been featured regularly in the Chinese press to provide her analysis of this process. She described the effects of China's policy as a "key, unstoppable dynamic globally." To bring this "Spirit of the Silk Road" to a Western audience, Zepp LaRouche has initiated a weekly Webcast, to counter the lying characterizations in the trans-Atlantic media of China's policy, and Xi's leadership. Only rarely can one find an honest report on China's dramatic accomplishments and its goals for the future.

"Most people are still unaware that we are at a crossroads of human history," she said in her first webcast, on October 5. If there were honest reporting on what China is doing, she continued, people would become excited, and would wish to be a part of this dynamic, which she calls a "New Paradigm for mankind." She spoke of the opportunity for this paradigm to advance when President Trump goes to Asia for a series of events, beginning on Nov. 5. He will meet with President Xi on Nov. 8.

A Bubble Is Not Economic Growth

One of the oft-repeated falsehoods about China's economy in the Western media is that credit expansion by Chinese financial institutions to fund the BRI projects has produced a financial bubble, which will ultimately pop. This argument, emanating from China's

Schiller Institute

Helga Zepp-LaRouche, leading a seminar in Beijing in 1996, calling for a Eurasian Development Bank and "an emergency meeting of the principal nation-state powers for the purpose of establishing a new international monetary system."

enemies, is based on classic neo-liberal dogma, which describes government spending as inherently wasteful, including spending channeled into infrastructure. This belief has played a major role in the failure of Western nations to invest in modernizing their own infrastructure, and is behind the incompetent insistence by neo-liberals that investment in infrastructure should be funded only by public-private partnerships, or PPPs, and further, that the choice of projects should be determined by their immediate profitability. As the federal government debt has grown in the United States to above $20 trillion—with the largest growth occurring under Presidents George W. Bush and Barack Obama—the adherents of this view now unabashedly argue that government credit for infrastructure is not possible, because of the large deficits already on the books. Instead of new investments to improve the economy, they push austerity, which in reality *decreases* productive economic activity and, therefore, physical wealth creation, as well as the creative powers of the citizens.

Ironically, those who argue that China's spending on the BRI has created a gigantic, unsupportable bubble, and that therefore Western governments should not emulate China in generating large volumes of credit for infrastructure, seem to have missed the fact that the biggest bubble in the world is not a Chinese bubble, but that which was created by the bailouts of banks and financial institutions in the trans-Atlantic world after the Crash of 2008. The quantitative easing (QE) policy of the central banks, which provided virtually zero-interest credit to those institutions, allowed them to continue carrying worthless debt on their books—which they continue to buy and sell—while pouring money into overvalued equity markets—stocks, bonds, and commodities. Thus, while spouting their "fiscal conservative, anti-government" rhetoric against government spending on infrastructure and science, they make exceptions when it comes to bailing out bankrupt financial institutions, so they may continue to run their speculative swindles!

As a result, the "too big to fail" (TBTF) banks today are larger than at the time of the 2008 crash; the biggest U.S. banks are 40% larger in assets. As there are now

Financial Times *of London warning of looming financial difficulties.*

fewer banks overall, there has been a concentration of banking assets held by a smaller number of institutions. Further, there has been an expansion of derivative positions, since efforts to rein in derivative trading failed. The Dodd-Frank banking "reform" bill did nothing to limit it—not surprising, as its sections on derivative trading were written by derivative traders! And with the volumes of cheap money flowing from the central banks to the TBTF banks, trading of financial instruments of dubious value has expanded, as traders are taking on more risk, in search of ever bigger profits.

Those economists, journalists, and politicians critical of China have, for the most part, until now, praised this bubble economy in the United States as "Obama's recovery," and lead the cheers, as stocks hit new record highs daily. But, as stock market valuations have soared "on a sea of liquidity," a real danger exists that, when the liquidity is removed, through "tightening," i.e., increasing interest rates, it will likely lead to a crash.

Crash Warnings Grow

A number of institutional voices in the trans-Atlantic world are now warning of the danger of a crash larger than 2008. El-Erian, chief economic adviser at Allianz, and former CEO of PIMCO, the world's largest bond trading firm, is one of them. In recent weeks both the International Monetary Fund (IMF) and the Bank for International Settlements (BIS) have sounded alarms over plans by central banks to raise interest rates and to divest themselves of the junk assets they took on their books as collateral for QE. In its Fall meeting in Washington, the IMF warned of "downside" risks, if central banks adopted a "faster-than-anticipated tightening," while the BIS in its annual survey identified what its economists called the "risky trinity": low productivity growth; unusually high debt levels; and limited room for political maneuver, given the growth of "populist" movements hostile to both the political and financial establishment.

Warnings from the European Union include a report by the Adam Smith Institute, "No Stress III: The Flaws in the Bank of England Stress Tests," which concludes that the "UK banking system is an accident waiting to happen." Another City of London insider, Ambrose Evans-Pritchard of the *Daily Telegraph*, wrote of the present economic conditions in the West, that he has "never seen a more dangerous confluence of circumstances, or more remarkable complacency." And, from Germany, the former German Finance Minister Wolfgang Schäuble, who had earlier played a large role in promoting the flow of liquidity coming from the European Central Bank to bail out the European Union's TBTF banks, has now told the *Financial Times* that he is concerned "about the increased risks arising from the accumulation of more and more liquidity and the growth of public and private debt."

On Oct. 16, President Trump's chief economic adviser, former Goldman Sachs President Gary Cohn, told the American Bankers Association that he is concerned that the clearinghouses that were set up under Dodd-Frank, allegedly to make derivative trading more "transparent," represent "a new systemic problem." The clearinghouses are supposed to guarantee payment if a derivative trading partner fails. But what happens, he asked, if a clearinghouse fails? He said that an estimated $278 trillion in interest-rate derivatives goes through clearinghouses. "These are just staggering numbers," he exclaimed, adding "We don't have a resolution plan for them."

These warnings all contain elements of a belated recognition of the dangers that the Western financial system now faces, but, at the same time, if people are trapped

swiss-image.ch/Photo by Remy Steinegger

Gary D. Cohn is concerned that clearinghouses that are suppposed to guarantee derivatives, could fail

inside a house that is on fire and realize that they are about to die in a deadly conflagration, this does not mean that they are intelligent, rational or know how to save themselves. Most of these financial "experts" refuse to accept self-blame, that it was they who stored open containers of flammable liquid next to an oil furnace. Today's neo-liberals, who created the policy of economic austerity and financial bailouts, such as Schäuble and the IMF, now warn of impending doom. What do they have to offer? Only more of the same—"stay the course," they say, "for the financial system must be saved," no matter how many people these policies kill.

LaRouche's Record

In the Oct. 20, 2017 issue of *Executive Intelligence Review*, an article written in 1996 by Lyndon LaRouche was republished, under the title "Why Are Nearly All Economists Quackademics?" In that article, LaRouche eviscerates the fraud and incompetence of the hegemonic monetarist theories—and those theories' spokesmen—which have governed the policies of Europe and America for the past forty-five years. A careful reading of that article shows conclusively that there are no financial sleight-of-hand tricks which could now save the banking system or stabilize the markets. An entirely new economic approach is required.

In 1971, LaRouche gained world renown when he forecast the imminent collapse of the post-World War II Bretton Woods system. Despite the fact that *all* leading economists—including Treasury secretaries, central bank heads, and college professors—dismissed LaRouche's warnings, he was proven right by the events of August 15 that year.

On October 19, 1987, U.S. stock markets had their biggest one-day drop in history, as a stock bubble popped. Four months earlier, Lyndon LaRouche forecast that there would be a stock crash *in October.*

Twenty years later, in July 2007, LaRouche warned of an impending collapse of the "Bush recovery," another speculative bubble, this time based on mortgage-backed securities trading in a market deregulated by the

1999 repeal of the Glass-Steagall bank separation act.

In both 1987 and 2007, LaRouche put forward as a solution the return to the American System of economics, beginning with a restoration of Glass-Steagall, to end government support for reckless speculation, combined with credit creation for investment in physical production. The system of credit, designed by the first Treasury Secretary of the United States, Alexander Hamilton, to secure investments in physical processes which would increase productivity, through a National Bank, is a central feature of the American System, which has been revived by LaRouche, and is included in his *Four New Laws*. It starts with the idea that there is a fundamental difference between credit which is invested to ensure productivity increases, which lifts up the whole economy, and debt creation, which only provides funds for gamblers and speculators, who expect to be bailed out when their bubble implodes, as it inevitably does.

Chinese Credit vs. Western Funny Money

Contrast the reality of the bankruptcy of the Western financial and economic system with the accelerating rate of growth of the *physical economy* in China, accomplished through improvements in productivity, which have resulted from BRI projects. While the central banks of the trans-Atlantic system have been churning out "funny money," to provide liquidity to banks that are *insolvent,* because of the worthless paper they are carrying on their books, and the unsustainable leverage they have generated, China's government credit agencies and its leading banks have been building the infrastructure platforms for the future, not only in China, but for its neighbors in Eurasia and in Africa.

The work on economic policy and theory done by Lyndon LaRouche, and by his wife Helga, is reflected in the success of the BRI of China, whose leaders clearly understand the principles embodied in LaRouche's Four Laws. This is the basis of the New Paradigm for which Mrs. LaRouche has been tirelessly campaigning, which has become an "unstoppable global dynamic" since Xi Jinping announced the BRI policy in 2013. It is now time to move mankind out from under the Old Paradigm, with its wars, terrorism, austerity, and bailouts, and for the United States and Europe to join this New Paradigm.

Learn the Lesson of Dec. 2, 1971

by Robert Ingraham

Oct. 20—In the Oct. 20, 2017 issue of *Executive Intelligence Review*, an article, written in 1996 by Lyndon LaRouche, was republished, under the title "Why Are Nearly All Economists Quackademics?" Given that we all now exist within a society increasingly driven by a "24-hour news cycle," and that millions of people are addicted to the hour-by-hour gossip that is spewed out from hundreds of "experts" and commentators, this would be an appropriate time to pause, and to reflect on a few of the observations made by LaRouche in that very insightful and accurate, short piece.

On any given day, or even any given hour, the average "consumer" of cyber-world news can now read wild predictions of an imminent financial crisis. This can take many different forms, from a "replay of the 2007-2008 crisis"; to the danger of a "1987-style stock market crash"; to a "collapse of the over-the-counter (OTC) derivatives market"; to a "failure of several too-big-to-fail banks." Like a stopped clock that tells the right time twice a day, several of these "predictions" obviously contain elements of partial truth, and the imminence and magnitude of the crisis we are now facing is staggering. But! Why would anyone accept the opinions of these "authorities"—be they central bank heads, Treasury secretaries, hedge fund managers, IMF officials, or sundry other economic commentators?

The overwhelming majority of those now making specific predictions of disaster are the very same people whose influence and policy proposals were responsible for creating the crisis we are now in. The shame of their years-long incompetence is a matter of public record. Axiomatically, they do not know how or why we got into this mess, and their solutions are absurd, if not outright evil. The hegemonic view among all of these utterly amoral individuals is oligarchical monetarism, where monetary profit takes priority over human lives.

At the same time, history does not repeat itself, and any analysis which begins by saying that we are going to have "another 2007-style crisis," or "another 1987-style crash," does not represents reality, but only the limited, linear mental processes of those making such utterances. The crisis we are now facing is much larger, more daunting, and far, far more dangerous than anything seen to date, and the steps taken to deal with it must start with a precise comprehension of the approach that is required.

Listen to LaRouche

On Dec. 2, 1971, at Queens College, New York, Lyndon LaRouche engaged in an hours-long debate with the noted economist Abba Lerner. Lerner had been chosen by the New York establishment to dis-

New York Stock Exchange.

Abba Lerner, speaking at a 1971 debate with Lyndon LaRouche (left), at Queens College, New York.

wrong. So why would you believe those failed Lilliputian voices today?

Lyndon LaRouche has advanced the **Science of Economics**, as that rigorous science was developed by Gottfried Leibniz, Alexander Hamilton, and others. It starts from the standpoint that human survival, a future for the human species, is only achievable through scientific discoveries and inventions, discoveries that increase mankind's power over nature, and that this increase in the productive power of humanity depends absolutely on an increase in the noëtic power of the population, such that the potential to make new discoveries is increased. The sole purpose of competent economic policy is to increase and accelerate that potential cognitive power. That defines human progress. It also defines the basis for sustained economic development. Any violation of that intention must lead to economic crisis and financial collapse.

credit LaRouche and to stop his growing influence, in the wake of LaRouche's uniquely singular and correct forecast of the collapse of the Bretton Woods Monetary System—a collapse which had occurred in August 1971—and one which no other leading economist had foreseen.

For our purposes here, what is notable about LaRouche's defeat of Lerner in that debate is not simply that he exposed the entire profession of leading establishment economists as incompetent fakesters and quackademics, but that he demonstrated that the economic policies which were mandated by those charlatans' choice of economic methods must lead to an adoption of outright fascist economic policies, policies which require a brutal rape and looting of the population, as carried out by Hitler's Finance Minister Hjalmar Schacht: Austerity, impoverishment and death.

The stunning fact of LaRouche's forecast of the 1971 collapse of the Bretton Woods Monetary System is that LaRouche was right, and **everybody else was wrong**—Nobel Prize economists, Treasury secretaries, bankers, and college professors—all of them were

A Reality Check

America now has a population of about 324 million people, of whom roughly 250 million are over the age of eighteen. According to the government's own (and usually conservative) figures, of that 250 million, about

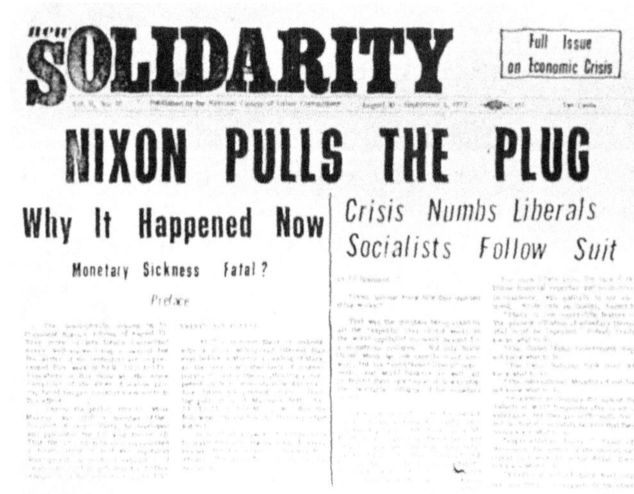

New Solidarity, *the LaRouche movement newspaper for many years, covering the end of the Bretton Woods system.*

A retail salesperson at a food hall in Plaza Hotel, New York City.

7 million are "officially" unemployed, another 95 million are "not in the labor force," and 35 million of the employed Americans earn less than $10.55 per hour. That's a total of 132 million Americans—more than half the adult population—who are barely subsisting, if that. Poverty is the new paradigm in the America produced by the prescriptions of the quackademics who took control of the nation's destiny—and advised every President—after 1971. The increase in the death rate, the drug epidemic, the suicides—these are now killing off millions of "useless eater" Americans: All this is a result of the hegemonic economic philosophy which has ruled the nation since 1971.

At the same time, energy use per capita, water use per capita and other physical-economic indicators have plummeted over the last 40 years. For example, there has been a 36% decrease in water consumption per capita since 1980. This includes not only water for people, but for industry, agriculture, and other vital needs. This destruction of the ability of the population to physically reproduce itself has been escalating, particularly under the Bush and Obama Presidencies. Today, among those who have jobs, 8 million are employed in the "financial sector," 16 million in "leisure, tourism, and hospitality," and 15 million in retail sales. America no longer has a productive work force capable of producing the next two to three generations.

During these recent decades, we have witnessed one after another quackademic win the Nobel Prize for economics—usually for devising a new mathematical formula to manipulate the money markets or a new behavioral approach to enforce Nazi "work makes you free" productivity schemes. The most urgent truth to be learned is that none of these idiots actually understand why we are in this crisis. They simply don't understand the science of human reproduction, as LaRouche always has. They are circling the ring of the Inferno inhabited by John von Neumann and Norbert Wiener.

There is no "financial" or "monetary" solution to this crisis. Granted, emergency measures must be taken, but as LaRouche specifies in the article referenced here, a competent economic recovery approach must include:

1. A universal Classical form of education for all young members of society.
2. Wage income must conform to what is necessary for the cultural level of an improved productive workforce.
3. Improvements in infrastructure, per-capita and per-square kilometer, must become a Characteristic Function of physical economy.
4. The rate of development in scientific and technological progress and Classical cultural development must also conform to the necessary Characteristic Function of physical economy.

The only additional requirement is to take the necessary financial and banking measures—utilizing Hamiltonian methods of National Banking—to put the old, sick, deranged, speculative monetary system out of its misery. Simply put it to sleep like a rabid dog now beyond all hope. End it.

This insistence, by LaRouche, that the **people** and the **rate of real physical economic development** are the only things that matter, is what none of the frauds who pass themselves off as financial experts can swallow. Forty years of immersion in linear quackademic nonsense has destroyed their reasoning.

Stop listening to the idle chatter from fools who know nothing about physical economy. Study LaRouche's Four Laws. Study the articles by LaRouche we are republishing in *EIR*. It is up to you.

Why Most Nobel Prize Economists Are Quacks

by Lyndon H. LaRouche, Jr.

This Economic Advisory was released on July 14, 1995.

Today, every nation on this planet is under the domination of a single, worldwide, monetary and financial system: the so-called International Monetary Fund (IMF) system. That system is about to go out of existence. The worst financial collapse of the Twentieth Century could erupt within as soon as weeks, or, in the unlikely case, the disintegration of the system could be postponed until as late as early 1997.

Nothing can save the present monetary and financial system. It could be gobbled up in an orderly bankruptcy reorganization conducted by governments, or, if governments are, as Hamlet said, too "pigeon-livered" to do this, it will reach the point that the system simply disintegrates within as short a span as 24 to 72 hours. That is to say, it would vanish as if in a cloud of smoke: in an implosion of what is called "reversed financial leverage."[1]

That information should come as no surprise; any competently trained economist would agree immediately with what has just been written here. They, and all honest mass news-media, would have been warning governments of this danger over years, even decades. To illustrate that point: The present writer has forecast just this danger—repeatedly, consistently, and accurately— during the past 30 years; during the mid-1970s, he found concurrence with his own forecast, on the general nature of the danger, in his personal meetings with such notable figures as the former economic adviser to President

The bankruptcy of "classroom mathematics": Radical positivist Niels Bohr, father of the Copenhagen School in physics, followed in the footsteps of the occultist Isaac Newton. This tradition has produced as many quacks in economic science as it has in physics and mathematics.

Charles de Gaulle, the distinguished Jacques Rueff. During the recent several years, another of the rare species of competent economist, France's Nobel Prize-winning economist, Maurice Allais,[2] has been warning publicly, and repeatedly of this imminent danger.

Yet, until a few months ago, most generally recognized economists, worldwide, showed themselves not competently trained. Until the aftermath of both the Orange County, California and Mexico outbreaks, they consistently derided such warnings—although, at that time, the symptoms of an onrushing, early general financial chain-reaction collapse, echoing the famous, Weimar Germany Reichsmark collapse of 1922-23, were already the dominant features of world markets.

---

1. A collapse best described by the same sets of equations used to describe a chemical or nuclear explosion.

2. See Maurice Allais, *Le Figaro*: April 26, May 9, June 1, and Nov. 15-16, 1994. Allais also has the special distinction, of being the only sane person yet to receive the Nobel Prize for Economics.

Now, over the course of the period since the Orange County bankruptcy and the Mexico crisis, a significant and increasing number of prominent economists and bankers nod sadly, and agree: The system is coming down. One might respond to that: Better late than never; should we not respond, instead: that the economics profession and the bankers have failed miserably over the past 25 years, or longer? Must we not say, that they should have foreseen this coming decades ago, and warned governments and the public of the consequence of continuing the mistaken policies already under way back then?

To recognize why otherwise educated and intelligent people, when confronted with generally accepted economics dogma, so often behave like credulous spectators at a carnival side-show, we must make clear certain deep-rooted false, empiricist, assumptions about science. These are the prevalent, mistaken assumptions which have shaped popular opinion on the subject of social theory in general and economics in particular. First, consider the subject-matter whose mention terrifies popular economic opinion today.

The facts just referenced pose three crucial questions of policymaking to the U.S.A.'s and other governments. 1) Why did virtually all of the most respected professional economists and bankers of the world fail so contemptibly, over a period of 30 years? 2) Why did we tolerate, over a period of 25 years, economic, monetary, and financial policies whose foreseeably inevitable consequence was a collapse of the physical economy of the planet, and also, inevitably, the worst monetary and financial collapse in European history since the mid-Fourteenth Century, when England set off the chain-reaction collapse of the Lombard debt-bubble of that time?[3] 3) Why do most governments of the world, and also most "popular opinion," support the policies of such transparently lunatic economic dogmas as those of former British Prime Minister Margaret Thatcher, Harvard's Prof. Jeffrey Sachs, Sen. Phil Gramm, and U.S. House Speaker Newt(on) Gingrich?

See Barbara Tuchman, *A Distant Mirror: The Calamitous Fourteenth Century* (New York: Alfred A. Knopf, 1978); also, Miriam Beard, *A History of The Businessman* (New York: MacMillan, 1938). Over the hundred years preceding that collapse of the "Lombard" debt-bubble, since the A.D. 1250 death of the Holy Roman Emperor Frederick II, Europe had been gripped by the rise of a Venice-controlled "Black Guelph" faction, and the effects of the invasion of Venice's ally, Genghis Khan's Mongols, from the east. By the time of the death of the anti-"Black Guelph" political leader, Dante Alighieri, all western Europe lay prostrate under the heel of Venice's "Black Guelph" agents, notably the ultra-usurious Lombard bankers—the, so to speak, Paul A. Volckers of their time. Miss Beard properly highlights the case of two of these swindlers, known by their French cognomens, "Biche" and "Mouche." Among the more disgusting cases of belated resistance to Venetian usury was England, which had been virtually a "suburban development project" of Venice's bankers since the relevant capitulations of comprador-kings Edward II and Edward III. Then, mid-century, came the time that the King of England, like the voters of Orange County, California more recently, repudiated England's debts to the Lombard House of Bardi, Biche's and Mouche's employer, and the entire banking system of Europe went promptly belly-up, in a chain-reaction of Fourteenth-Century "reversed financial leverage."

---

1. The Present Economic Crisis

Before attempting to answer the series of questions we have just posed, consider the relevant most crucial facts about the presently skyrocketting, global, financial and economic crisis. The data upon which the following summary is premised are the standard statistics publicly available to every government and leading economist in the world.

---

3. See Barbara Tuchman, *A Distant Mirror: The Calamitous Fourteenth Century* (New York: Alfred A. Knopf, 1978); also, Miriam Beard, *A History of The Businessman* (New York: MacMillan, 1938). Over the hundred years preceding that collapse of the "Lombard" debt-bubble, since the A.D. 1250 death of the Holy Roman Emperor Frederick II, Europe had been gripped by the rise of a Venice-controlled "Black Guelph" faction, and the effects of the invasion of Venice's ally, Genghis Khan's Mongols, from the east. By the time of the death of the anti-"Black Guelph" political leader, Dante Alighieri, all western Europe lay prostrate under the heel of Venice's "Black Guelph" agents, notably the ultra-usurious Lombard bankers—the, so to speak, Paul A. Volckers of their time. Miss Beard properly highlights the case of two of these swindlers, known by their French cognomens, "Biche" and "Mouche." Among the more disgusting cases of belated resistance to Venetian usury was England, which had been virtually a "suburban development project" of Venice's bankers since the relevant capitulations of comprador-kings Edward II and Edward III. Then, mid-century, came the time that the King of England, like the voters of Orange County, California more recently, repudiated England's debts to the Lombard House of Bardi, Biche's and Mouche's employer, and the entire banking system of Europe went promptly belly-up, in a chain-reaction of Fourteenth-Century "reversed financial leverage."

The decline of the U.S. market basket

	1960	1963	1966	1970	1980	1990
Capital goods						
Fertilizer	2.00	1.75	1.39	1.29	1.36	1.26
Construction machinery	1.00	0.93	0.83	0.97	1.19	1.84
Mining machinery	1.46	1.72	1.48	1.53	2.18	3.00
Oilfield machinery	1.28	1.25	1.17	1.03	1.27	1.61
Industrial construction	1.38	1.38	0.86	1.31	1.41	2.65
Ocean-going shipping	0.30	0.24	0.99	0.07	0.06	1.05
Household goods						
Textiles	0.89	0.88	0.92	1.25	2.26	2.90
Shoes, leather	0.86	0.90	0.95	1.17	1.97	3.26
Passenger cars produced	1.14	1.05	0.97	1.30	1.51	1.74
Residential construction	1.16	0.90	1.16	0.96	1.03	1.14
School construction	1.12	1.17	0.98	1.28	2.69	2.00
Hospital construction	1.67	0.97	1.09	0.91	1.38	1.20
Intermediate goods						
Copper	26.03	28.54	22.85	19.81	29.06	22.17
Nickel	0.94	1.09	0.99	0.87	1.25	52.89
Bauxite	4.75	6.98	13.01	11.63	17.71	65.26
Hydraulic cement	3.87	3.97	3.77	3.89	4.29	3.68
Crude steel	1.76	1.93	1.62	1.71	2.24	1.74
Natural sulfur	3.57	4.05	3.52	3.63	4.54	8.44

This table shows the relationship to a 1967 standard, of a selection of capital goods, household goods, and intermediate goods which are part of thge market basket of consumption of the U.S. economy. The numbers are calculated based upon the greater of consumption or production, then indexed to 1967. The number in the table, represents the number by which the consumption in that year should be multiplied, to meet the 1967 market basket standard. Figures over 1.00 show a shortfall, while figures under 1.00 show a surplus.

For example, for fertilizer consumption in 1990 to have met the 1967 standard, consumption would need to have been 1.26 times actual cosumption.

Source: EIR market basket studies

To those statistics apply the following procedures, for the purpose of comparing U.S. per-capita income and output during the interval 1956-94. Reduce the publicly available data used, to the form of values expressed as quantities per capita,[4] per family household, and per square kilometer of relevant land-use.

Define input as consumption by persons, by households, by agriculture, by mining, by basic economic infrastructure, by manufacturing, by construction, and by allowable ratios of employment for sales and administrative functions of both government and the private sector. Use U.S. data for 1956 as the standard of comparison for "allowable ratios of employment for sales and administration of both government and the private sector." (See **Table 1.**) This yields "market baskets of consumption" for persons, households, infrastructure, production, and sales and administration: all, of course, per capita, per family household, and per square kilometer of relevant land-use.

Define output as the production of the items contained in the market-baskets of consumption.

The content of these market-baskets is limited to useful physical goods, measured in physical (not monetary) units, plus three elements of infrastructure indispensable for maintaining and improving the demographic characteristics of the family household, and for maintaining and improving the productive powers of labor: education, health-care delivery, and science and technology as such.[5]

The assessment of these market-basket requirements is implicit. The relevant question is, what would be the actuarial impact upon demographic characteristics of family households and productivity (ratio of output to input of these market-basket contents), were the contents of some among the total spectrum of market-baskets to be increased, or decreased? Define "implicit economic equilibrium" as a secular trend corresponding to

---

4. I.e., per capita of total available labor-force.

5. For example, to maintain the net rate of growth of physical productivity (per capita of total available labor-force, per family household, and per square kilometer of relevant land-area) at circa 1963 levels, approximately 5% of the total labor-force must be employed in functions of physical science and engineering. This references the comparison of three bench-mark, developed economies (the U.S.A., Germany, and Japan) for the interval 1967-70. If the level of employment for technological progress, and in related machine-tool sector categories, drops below that ration, the economy will suffer an entropic physical-economic net decline.

Employment Of Operatives as Percentage of Actual Requirement

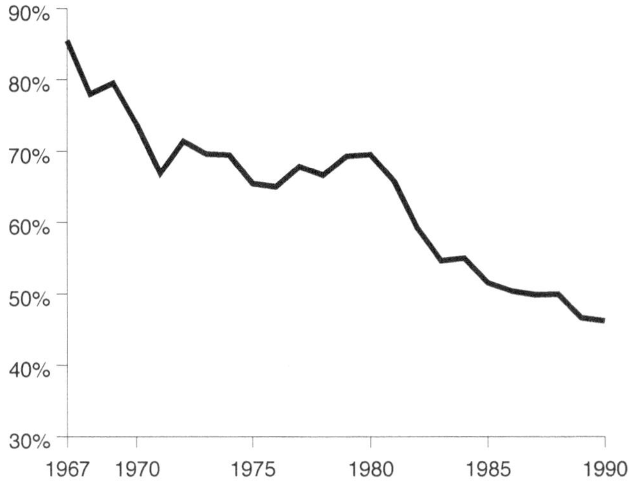

Percent of Actual Workforce Required To Produce 1967-Style Market Basket

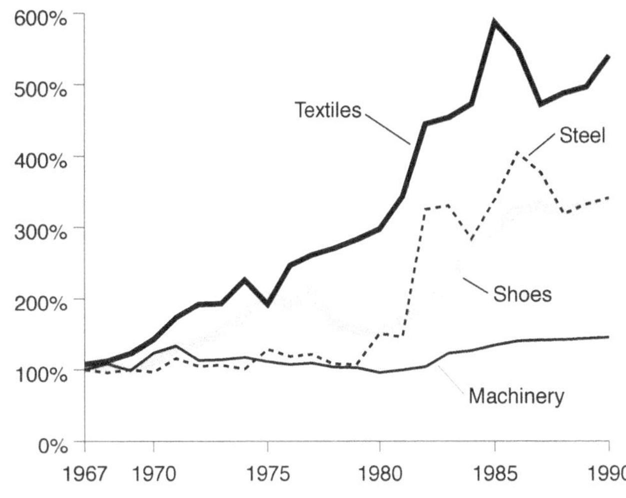

a rate of physical economic growth, measured in terms of demographics and output-to-input ratios, of about 5% (physical-economic) growth per annum.

Employ the suggestive imageries of the undergraduate science classroom; identify that "implicit equilibrium" level as representing the "energy of the system" of the physical-economic process at that interval of the continuing process. Thus, continuing to employ the same symbolism: The ratio of output to input, implicitly defines a ratio of "free energy" to "energy of the system."[6] This symbolism requires us to state that the healthy, non-degenerative ("sustainable") phases of an economic process, are *characteristically* "not-entropic."[7]

By that standard, using nothing other than the official statistics which are generally available to all professionals and relevant governmental and private institutions: The U.S. economy has been in a continuing state of physical-economic decline over the entire period, from 1967-70 to 1992-95.[8] (See **Figures 1-3.**)

---

6. Do not overlook a crucial point implied here. What does society do with the "free energy" margin? A sane society reinvests most of it not only for expanding the economy in scale, but also in increasing the relative content of the energy-of-the-system, per capita, per household, and per square kilometer. Thus, the capital-intensity and power-density requirements of a "sustainable" economic process are continually increased. To maintain a "constant" minimum ratio of "free energy" to "energy of the system" over successive epochs of the process, requires a corresponding increase in the physical margin of output available for investment. This latter constraint is satisfiable by no other means than advances in productive and related technologies. The same challenge is presented by the apparent relative finiteness of what an existing level of technology regards as required natural resources; this constraint can be overcome solely through the same means: advances in productive and related technologies.

7. The system is actually "not-entropic," not merely in the symbolic, but the strictly physical sense. "Not-entropy" is employed here in a sense distinct from Prof. Norbert Wiener's silly derivation of his term "negentropy" from Ludwig Boltzmann's H-theorem (Norbert Wiener, *Cybernetics* [New York: John Wiley & Sons, 1948]; see Morris Levitt, "Linearity and Entropy: Ludwig Boltzmann and the Second Law of

Thermodynamics," *Fusion Energy Newsletter,* September 1976, pp. 3-18). The measure of the not-entropy of a system is implicitly supplied by the mathematician Georg Cantor (n.b., *Beiträge zur Begründung der Mannigfaltigkeitslehre,* in *Georg Cantor: Gesammelte Abhandlungen mathematischen und philosophischen Inhalts* [Berlin-Heidelberg: Springer-Verlag, 1990], pp. 282-356). The mathematical representation of the relative not-entropy of a physical process is effected through a comparative study of a increase in the relative cardinalities of two crucially distinct successive states of a system: e.g., the implicit increase of the density of implicitly enumerable mathematical discontinuities per arbitrarily chosen interval of action of the process. The cause for a "sustainable" increase in the productive powers of labor, in a physical economy, is the realized increase in those forms of knowledge (i.e., cumulative discoveries of valid principle) which produce *the effect of* technological progress. This function for "not-entropy" was discovered by the present writer during the course of a project (1948-52), prompted by a determination to expose the fraud of Wiener's fraudulent claim to represent human knowledge by the mechanical means of statistical "information theory." The present writer employed Cantor's work to illuminate certain deeper implications of Bernhard Riemann's 1854 habilitation dissertation, "On The Hypotheses Which Underlie Geometry," (*Über die Hypothesen, welche der Geometrie zu Grunde liegen,* in *Bernhard Riemann's Gesammelte Mathematische Werke,* Heinrich Weber, editor [New York: Dover Publications, Inc., 1953], pp. 272-287). Hence, the application of Riemann's work to solve the problem of adequate representation of the function earlier defined by this writer, became known by the seemingly anomalous, but descriptively accurate "LaRouche-Riemann Method."

8. See Christopher White, "NAM's 'Renaissance' of U.S. Industry: It

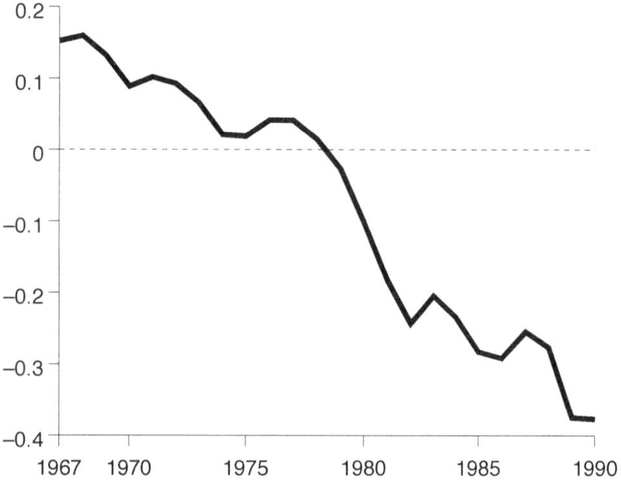

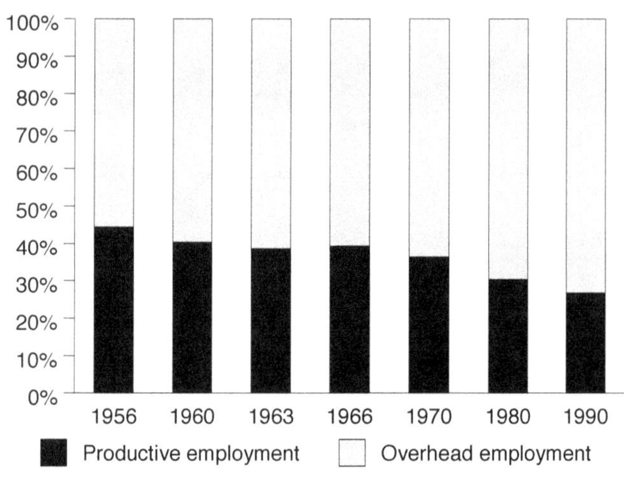

Sources: *Historical Statistics of the United States,* Bureau of the Census, 1975; Department of Labor, Occupational Employment Division, and Bureau of Labor Statistics, *Monthly Labor Review*; Department of Education, National Library of Education; Department of Health and Human Services, Bureau of Health Professions; American Nurses Association.

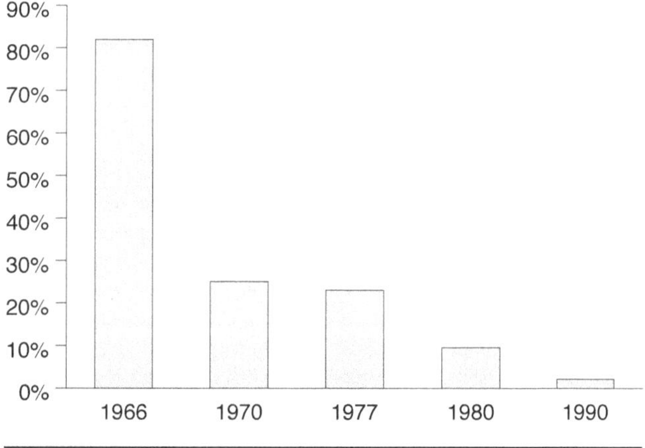

Sources: Bank for International Settlements surveys (1986, 1989, 1992); U.S. Federal Reserve surveys (1977, 1980, 1983); GATT.

Overall, the relevant available statistics are sufficient to show, that the same trend is characteristic of the world-economy taken as a whole. The same array of statistics shows, that although there were tendencies in this disastrous direction in the U.S.A. prior to 1963, it was a package of radical policy-changes set into motion during the 1964-72 interval, which has been responsible for the persisting net decline of the entire world's physical economy since 1972.

During the 1972-95 period to date, the percentile of the total labor-force employed in producing what we have identified, above, as "energy of the system," has been successively shrunken (see **Figure 4**), while the physical productivity of the labor still employed in these categories has also been successively shrunken over this same interval (see Figure 2).[9] This has been true in the U.S.A.; it is also, if even more emphatically, the case for the planet taken as a whole.

Next, compare the physical-economic developments and trends with the corresponding arrays of monetary and financial data. Begin with the simplest comparison: shifting patterns in the ratio of foreign trade to foreign-exchange turnover. After that, turn to the internal mechanisms of finance itself.

In 1976, the import-export trade of the U.S.A. ac-

counted for a reported 23% of the total daily U.S. foreign-exchange turnover. Following the disastrous initial impact of the lunatic October 1979 policy changes introduced by Federal Reserve Chairman Paul A. Volcker, by 1981, the trade factor in foreign exchange turnover had dropped to about 5% (see **Figure 5**). By 1992,

---

Never Happened," *EIR,* April 14, 1995.

9. Ibid. See, also, Christopher White, "LaRouche's Ninth Economic Forecast—One Year Later," *EIR,* July 7, 1995.

under President George Bush, the figure had dropped to less than 2%; for mad Margaret Thatcher's Britain, the figure had dropped to about half of 1%, and the world average had declined to about 2%. Today, taking into account "off-balance-sheet" derivatives transactions, it is safe to say, without fear of exaggerating the case, that total world trade accounts for less than 1% of daily world financial turnover.

In sum: The world's monetary and financial systems have been "de-coupled" from the real economy. Officially reported "economic growth" is a hoax, for two very obvious principal reasons. First, Gross National Product/Gross Domestic Product estimates, the figures used to report putative economic growth, are based on estimates of *monetary* Value Added; therefore, since the monetary-financial system has been de-coupled from the real economy, GNP and GDP estimates, even if they were honestly compiled, have a corresponding degree of irrelevance to any discussion of national economic health. Second, of course, governments and related agencies lie—with greater abandon, each passing year—in every statistical analysis of this sort.[10]

That de-coupling of money and finance from real economy is built into the changes in policy-shaping trends of the past 30 years: since the so-called "cultural paradigm-shift," which began as an orchestrated mass sociological phenomenon during 1964. The anti-science (anti-rationalist), "post-industrial," and "neo-Malthusian" trends introduced into the fevered, sex-crazed, and pot-soaked brains of (admittedly only) a majority among campus-based anti-war protesters during the 1964-72 interval, are exemplary of this part of the problem.[11] From about 1966, the London Tavis-

tock Institute's influence succeeded in forcing initial major cutbacks in the U.S. science-driver (space) program, arguing that the success of space projects had inspired too many Americans with a deplorable liking for not only science, but also rationality in general.[12] The same year, the first neo-Malthusian proposal for making population control an issue of U.S. foreign policy was introduced into the U.S. State Department.[13] During that period, Rep. George Bush (R-Tex.) earned the nickname of "Rubbers" for his zealous prosecution of the cause of birth control.[14] By 1967, Zbigniew Brzezinski contributed his own "New Age" epiphany: his conversion from Christianity to the "Third Wave,"[15] to Norbert Wiener's, Robert Theobald's, Alvin Toffler's, and looney Lord William Rees-

---

product of Bertrand Russell crony Robert M. Hutchins's Center for the Study of Democratic Institutions. What is recognized as the "rock" cult-fad spread since that 1964 appearance of the Beatles, was a joint creation of satan-cultist Aleister Crowley's followers and the "wise guy" financier interests of the recording and concert mafia. Even a decade and a half earlier than 1964, through his fight against the irrationalist cult-dogma of "information theory," this writer was already familiar with the establishment circles who played a key role in steering the anti-civilization cultural-paradigm shift of the 1960s and 1970s. In Boston, this featured Air Force- and RAND-funded projects at MIT's RLE; in the New York City Metropolitan area, this circle of plotters was typified by a series of seminars convened under the sponsorship of the Josiah Macy, Jr. Foundation. The latter included prominent associates of MK-Ultra's Gregory Bateson, and his sometime-wife, Dame Margaret Mead. See *Dope, Inc.* (Washington, D.C.: Executive Intelligence Review, 1992) for the links among MK-Ultra, et al., and the circles which organized the mid-1960s mass-distribution of LSD-25 to university campuses around the U.S.A. Margaret Mead and MK-Ultra's Gregory Bateson, for example, were associates of Bertrand Russell and Robert M. Hutchins, in the 1938 launching, at the University of Pennsylvania, of the Unification of the Sciences project, one of the principal anti-science feeder conduits into the post-World War II launching of the "New Age" counter-culture.

12. See the London Tavistock Institute's "Rapaport report" on the effects of the U.S. space program.

13. Anticipating U.S. Secretary of State Henry A. Kissinger's overtly genocidal policy-outline of 1974, *National Security Study Memorandum-200: Implications of Worldwide Population Growth for U.S. Security and Overseas Interests,* Dec. 10, 1974 (unpublished: available in the National Archives, Washington, D.C.).

14. See "Rubbers Goes to Congress," pp. 186-213 of Webster G. Tarpley and Anton Chaitkin, *George Bush: The Unauthorized Biography* (Washington, D.C.: Executive Intelligence Review, 1992).

15. Cf. Zbigniew Brzezinski, *Between Two Ages: America's Role in the Technetronic Era,* Prepared Under the Auspices of the Research Institute on Communist Affairs, Columbia University (New York: Viking Press, 1970).

---

10. On massive fraud in official economic-growth reports and quarterly forecasts by the Federal Reserve System and U.S. Department of Labor, see Lyndon H. LaRouche, Jr.'s Democratic presidential-nomination campaign TV address of Feb. 4, 1984: "Stopping the Worldwide Economic Collapse," published by The LaRouche Democratic Campaign in *A Program For America,* 1985.

11. The two most exemplary of influential events of 1964, are the publishing of Robert Theobald's *The Triple Revolution* and the staging of the imported "Beatles" on CBS's "Ed Sullivan Show." That book was, together with Rachel Carson's fraudulent *Silent Spring* (New York: Houghton Mifflin, 1962), the opening salvo in the effort to launch a mass-based anti-technology movement under the rubric of "post-industrial society." (As Environmental Protection Agency head William Ruckelshaus admitted, in ordering the virtual banning of DDT, his decision to capitulate to Rachel Carson's dupes on this issue, was a political decision, in defiant disregard of the scientific evidence supplied to his committee.) *The Triple Revolution* was a Ford Foundation-lubricated

Mogg's neo-paganist[16] cult of "information theory."[17]

These and related mass-brainwashing efforts prepared the way for the crucial event of the 1964-72 transition to a "New Age": the Aug. 15-16, 1971 decisions of the U.S. Nixon Administration, de-coupling the U.S. dollar from the Bretton Woods gold-reserve standard. That decision established, preemptively, a worldwide "floating exchange-rate" monetary order, to replace the pro-industrial monetary system contracted at Bretton Woods.

The original Bretton Woods agreements were formally broken at the Azores monetary conference of 1972. The 1973-74 "oil-price shock," conducted by Britain's London petrolem-marketing cartel, with assistance from U.S. Secretary of State (and British agent of influence) (Sir) Henry A. Kissinger,[18] either wrecked or severely damaged the industrial economies of the world, including that of the U.S.A. The effects of the London "oil-price shock" caper, led to the Rambouillet monetary conference of 1975, at which the looting of economies through "floating exchange-rate" speculation was apotheosized as an immortal god of IMF Olympus.

____

16. See Lord William Rees-Mogg, "Dogmatic Without Dogma: Many of the New Forms of Religion Are Breaking Away from Hierarchies in the Search for Authenticity," London *Times,* July 13, 1995. Rees-Mogg is a devotee of Alvin Toffler's "Third Wave," and a leading backer of U.S. House of Representatives Speaker Newt(on) Gingrich. He is also a vilely hateful enemy, together with Conrad Black's London *Telegraph,* and the *American Spectator,* of U.S. President Bill Clinton.

17. Lord Rees-Mogg has proposed that 95% of the population should receive no education at all. He has proposed that the educated 5%, creating Alvin Toffler's "information" in isolated places, such as perhaps the islands of the English Channel, will supply the future world all the needed wealth of a global "Third Wave" utopia.

18. There is a continuing, hysterically lying effort from high-level mass news-media and other circles, to deny the conclusive evidence, that former U.S. Secretary of State Henry Kissinger has been, officially, an agent of influence of the British foreign-intelligence service during more than 50 years to date, since early days in Wilton Park training, at Harvard. See Henry A. Kissinger, "Reflections on a Partnership: British and American Attitudes to Postwar Foreign Policy," official transcript of his keynote address delivered on the occasion of the 200th anniversary of the founding of the British foreign service by Jeremy Bentham, delivered at Chatham House (Royal Institute for International Affairs), May 10, 1982 (Washington, D.C.: Center for Strategic and International Studies, 1982): "In my White House incarnation then [1969-77], I kept the British Foreign Office better informed and more closely engaged than I did the American State Department...." The Harvard Wilton Park unit under British agent of influence William Yandell Elliot, Kissinger's trainer, is a subsidiary of British foreign intelligence's Chatham House. For an elaboration of the treasonous mind-set which Kissinger acquired at Harvard's Wilton Park unit, see Henry A. Kissinger, *A World Restored: Metternich, Castlereagh and the Problems of Peace 1812-1822* (Boston: Houghton Mifflin, 1957).

The next decisive development leading into the presently onrushing collapse, occurred 1979. In spring of that year, while campaigning[19] for nomination as the new U.S. Federal Reserve Chairman, Paul A. Volcker announced that he considered "controlled disintegration of the [world] economy" an acceptable policy for an incoming Fed chairman. Those words, and Volcker's later practice as Fed chairman, echoed the proposals detailed by Fred Hirsch in the New York Council on Foreign Relations 1975-76 *Project 1980s* outline of policies being specified for the incoming administration of President Jimmy Carter; Carter appointees Cyrus Vance and Zbigniew Brzezinski had been key project coordinators for that CFR policy-planning. Beginning October 1979, Fed Chairman Volcker applied Hirsch's "controlled disintegration of the economy" with full and sudden force: zooming prime interest-rates into the stratosphere of usury, way above the rate of profit available in any known honest form of business enterprise. Since the ruinous effects of the 1979-83 implementation of Volcker's measures, there has been an increasing rate of net flow of financial and real (physical) capital, out of the productive sector, into the realm of pure financier speculation.

The Volcker measures, together with two disastrous, additional pieces of legislative lunacy, the St Germain-Garn and Gramm-Rudman bills, sent the U.S. economy on a reeling, "junk bond" orgy of financial looting and speculation, through 1982-87. The October 1987 stock-market collapse signalled the coming end of the "junk bond" phase, and inaugurated that "financial derivatives" bubble which has made the early doom of the existing monetary system inevitable.

To complete the sketch, showing why the early collapse of the system, during the coming months, is now inevitable, examine the ironies of the derivatives bubble itself.

At the core, what is called, euphemistically, "investment" in the financial-derivatives form of "futures," is somewhat less reputable than gambling at the tables of a Monte Carlo or Las Vegas casino. It has been fairly described, repeatedly, by Maurice Allais as a casino economy.[20] On at least two public occasions, prominent Japanese officials have described "derivatives" as "financial AIDS" in the world monetary and financial sys-

____

19. In Britain, naturally.

20. Cf. Maurice Allais, *loc. cit.*

tem.[21] I have often referenced the fact that "derivatives" in the financial-economic realm is analogous to the model of cancer presented in one of my old textbooks, that of the mathematical biophysicist Nicholas Rashevsky.[22]

Typical is the case of the gamble which tumbled the famous Lord Shelburne's Barings bank into bankruptcy earlier this year. It happened at Barings branch office in Singapore, currently one of the world's leading centers of financial prostitution. Their man there placed multibillion-dollar bets—not investments, but out-and-out crap-shoot-style side-bets—on the short-term outcome of shifts in both the Tokyo stock and bond markets. It was an enterprise steeped in the fiscal prudence of a New York City numbers-racket runner. Barings lost the bet on the numbers, and tumbled into bankruptcy as a result of that, plus other gambling losses. Derivatives speculation is gambling, on a thin margin, often risking large amounts of other people's financial assets. The Seventeenth Century's John-Law-style South Sea and Mississippi bubbles were paragons of fiscal conservativism, by contrast.

For purposes of practice, the most notable difference between today's wild-eyed Singapore, City of London, or Wall Street Yuppie, hedging derivatives

The main difefrence between today's Yuppie brokers and derivatives traders, and the Seventeenth Century financial bubblers,is that the latter did not have personal computers and high-speed,round-the world,round-the-clock communications links.

bets, and the Seventeenth Century financial bubblers, is that John Law's acquaintances did not have modern personal computers and high-speed, round-the-world, round-the-clock communications links. The application of a blend of John Von Neumann's Theory of Games[23] and Chaos Theory[24] to these modes of calculation and communication, permits a rate of speculative chain-reactions, subsuming impulses momentarily approaching near-light-speeds. This not only permits, but fosters rates of speculative inflation never before even imagined.

There are three most essential "mechanisms" of the resulting, worldwide financial bubble: 1) The numerically largest factor involved is the magnitude of the

---

21. In 1990, former Japan Finance Minister Tomichi Hashimoto (currently trade minister) described as "financial AIDS" the policies which President Bush and Mrs. Thatcher were urging, not only for Japan, but for all Asian countries. On June 19, 1995, a Japan source informed Executive Intelligence Review News Service, Inc., that "seeking a cure for 'financial AIDS' was on the agenda in June 18-19 talks between Japan Prime Minister Tomiichi Murayama and his cabinet, and President Jacques Chirac and European Union officials."

22. Nicholas Rashevsky, *Mathematical Biophysics* (Chicago: University of Chicago, 1938). The featuring of this usage of "financial cancer" by my friend Jacques Cheminade, in his 1995 campaign for election as President of France, caused an epoch-making outburst of lunacy from leading Paris media.

23. John Von Neumann and Oskar Morgenstern, *The Theory of Games and Economic Behavior,* 3rd edition (Princeton, N.J.: Princeton University Press, 1953).

24. So-called "chaos theory" is a fanciful piece of pseudoscience-fiction derived from a misunderstanding of the flawed work on infinite series by Newton, Newton-devotees Leonhard Euler, Augustin Cauchy, et al. Starting from adoption of Newton's famous Latin motto, *"et Hypotheses non fingo,"* the remarkable assumption is made, that the mathematical discontinuity axiomatically inhering in the inconsistency among mutually-exclusive mathematical-physical theorem-lattices can be bridged "at infinity." Thus, did Cauchy set out to circumcise Leibniz's calculus, and, in his blundering enthusiasm, castrated it, instead.

A New Era for Human Civilization

"notional" (fictitious) capital values, which are treated as the equivalent of money-capital for the purposes of the derivatives form of futures speculation; 2) the second largest factor is the flow of monetary stimulus into the maelstrom of financial speculation, in derivatives and related categories; 3) the speculative bubble's root-dependency upon an income-stream of real wealth taken out of real consumption and the production cycle. To determine why and how a bubble will pop, and to estimate when it will probably pop, one must focus upon the function of these combined, interacting three mechanisms.

Since the typical layman has no notion of the meaning or functional significance of the term, "fictitious capital," two clarifying illustrations are supplied here: first, the treatment of a simplified representation of what occurs as speculative appreciations (nominal "capital gains") in secondary stock-transactions, and, second, a similar case in speculation in New York slum-rental real estate during the 1960s. To understand how "derivatives" speculation balloons, and then, inevitably, collapses in a sudden, "nuclear-like" implosion, it is sufficient to carry the ordinary image of purely parasitical speculation, as seen in secondary stock-markets and slum rental real-estate properties, into that domain of which is the "derivatives" form of numbers-racketeering.

The first example: A man has 100 shares of common stock in Widgets, Inc., which he has purchased from that company's representative for $100 a share: $10,000. At that time, the stock's expected annual dividend-income is $5 per share. Meanwhile, a subsequent fluctuation in the prevailing interest increases the relative financial advantage in a financial speculator's holding of that $5 yield per share. As a result, traders are willing to pay $102 a share, instead of $100, for a share of Widget common. The $2 gain in price is purely fictitious, purely speculative, rather than the result of some action related to investment within the production cycle as such. The speculative gain of $2 a share is, as such, a purely financial phenomenon, not an economic one.

Continuing the same example, go to the next step in the hierarchy of speculation. Let a trading company be incorporated whose sole source of income is fictitious capital gains of the type represented by the indicated $2 gain in Widget common stock. Let this company issue stock. Paid-in capital put to one side, the remaining assets which secure the value of that latter stock are already purely fictitious, rather than real-economic assets.

Let the price of a share of that stock be $100, and let the expected dividend be $5 per year. Fluctuations in the value of that stock now represent fictitious values based upon appreciations, or depreciations of what are already purely fictitious values.

The second example, the case of the Manhattan slum-rental property, affords a more intimate view of the essential morbidity of fictitious gains in general. During the relevant period cited, the rule-of-thumb market valuation of a Manhattan rental property was calculated as a mutiple of the expected annual rental income. Thus, a landlord, by using various devices to increase the rental rate per square foot, could increase the nominal market value of a savagely deteriorating property. This was characteristic of slum rental properties in New York City during that time.[25]

The intrinsic value of the building used as an investment in slum rental property was almost an irrelevance, except as the physical structure provided a means for parking a relatively large number of rent-paying families on a city lot no larger than the standard plot allowed, during the 1920s or 1930s, for an urban single or two-family occupancy in a typical "working-class residential district" in a city such as Lynn, Massachusetts. Under the indicated slum-rental investment arrangements for Manhattan, the greater part of the paid-in rental income represented nothing other than "feudal" ground-rent, the latter a purely fictitious sort of economic value. Thus, the physical purchasing-power of the capitalized value of the slum could be zooming skyward, while the physical value of the building itself were falling rapidly toward zilch. The fluctuations in the financial value of the investment in the rental property had been "de-coupled" from the economic value of building and its use.

Thus, companies which speculated in fictitious gains from such investments could capitalize their fictitious earnings (capital gains) from the turnover in a number of such slum-investments, creating what we shall label Exhibit A. Let the profit of operations involving Exhibit A be labelled Exhibit B. This poses the question: What would a financial speculator pay to own the right to collect the expected annual dividend labelled Exhibit B? Suppose that prospective buyer expects a 10% financial return annually; in that case, the ownership of the right to collect Exhibit B annually

---

25. See Paul Gallagher, "How New York's Slumlords Created a Financial Bubble," *New Federalist,* Feb. 13, 1995.

would be approximately ten times the price of Exhibit B: creating Exhibit C.

These two examples introduce the principled features of the kind of process upon which all financial speculation in general is based. Financial derivatives represent the shifting of this sort of speculation from investment to pure betting, sometimes called "hedging." The point of these two, admittedly much simplified illustrations, is to identify the role of unreal, i.e., fictitious values, in feeding a bubble: as Exhibit A feeds Exhibit B, which feeds Exhibit C. What gives the financial bubble its specific quality is that without the growth of successive tiers of pure speculation (fictitious appreciation), the growth of the bubble comes to a standstill.

At the point of standstill, investors are in a scramble to sell out from under the collapse of the bubble as a whole; the scramble becomes a panic. Consider a panic operating globally, at computer speeds, along pathways of contemporary cable and satellite communications: The panic zooms, hyperbolically, into a "reversed-leverage" analog of a thermonuclear explosion: an implosion which causes the disintegration of virtually every financial and central-banking monetary institution of the planet, within a lapsed time of hours, 48 to 72 hours at most.

The maintenance of the growth of financial speculation requires an inflow of primary monetary aggregates (e.g., Federal Reserve issues of U.S. dollars) into the network of financial speculation. The multiplier-effect embedded within the tiered structure of the speculative bubble demands such money in quantities which are only a fraction of the rate at which new fictitious aggregates are being generated within the bubble, but the inflow of that currency-issue is crucial for the continued existence of the bubble-process as a whole. That leverage is the second of the principal mechanisms to be considered.

The inflow of currency into the bubble generates a tax upon the real economy. In part, this is literally a "tax," expressed in the form of government debt-service payments against the growing mass of debt used by the central banks to generate the flow of money into the bubble. Since the bubble is leveraged against outflows of real value from the productive cycle, among other sources, and since the mechanism of the bubble is leveraged borrowing, the growth of the bubble is reflected in accumulated financial charges embedded in every pore of the society's economic life. This is the

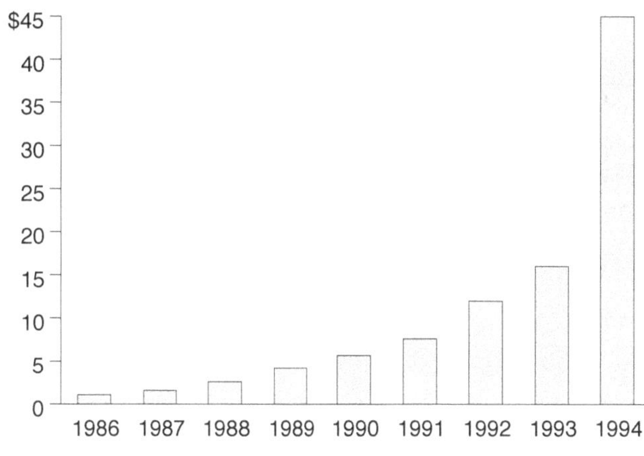

Source: Bank for International Settlements.

third of the principal mechanisms to be considered.

In summary, the functional interrelationship among the three mechanisms, is this. The increase of the size of the bubble increases the rate of growth of fictitious accumulations required to prevent the bubble from shifting into a reversed-leverage phase. The increase of the rate of growth of fictitious accumulations required, obliges the central banking systems to feed increased money-flows into the bubble's speculative base, otherwise, the fictitious accumulations are slowed, and the bubble as a whole then shifts into a reversed-leverage phase. The increase of the accumulated debt-capitalization used to fund the inflows of currency into the bubble's speculative base, causes an increased tax (of various sorts) upon the economy which the central banking system is looting to support the speculative base of the bubble.

Consider the charts and graphs reflecting the statistical studies of Christopher White, John Hoefle, Anthony Wikrent, et al. in that light (**Figures 6-8**).

1) Over the interval from the base reference period of 1967-70, until 1990-95, the physical-economic consumption and output of the U.S. economy, per capita, have nearly halved. At present, the decline is accelerating significantly.

2) Over the interval 1976-92, the percentile of U.S. foreign-exchange turnover represented by import-export trade had fallen from 23% to about 2%. Today, taking into account both reported and estimated rates of off-bal-

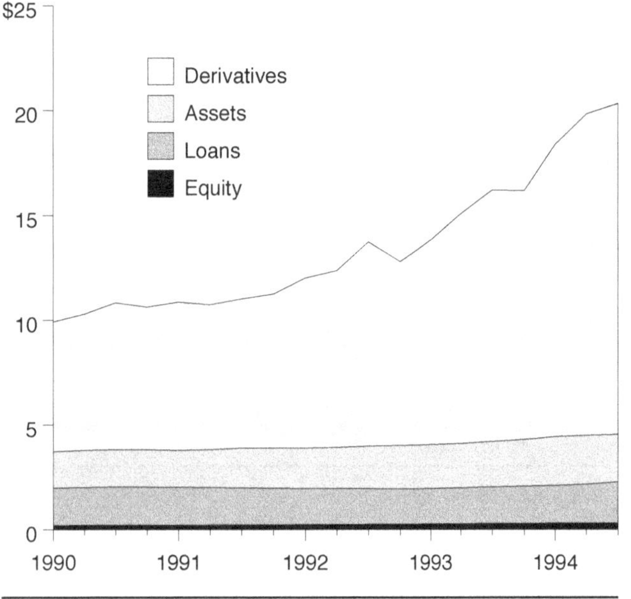

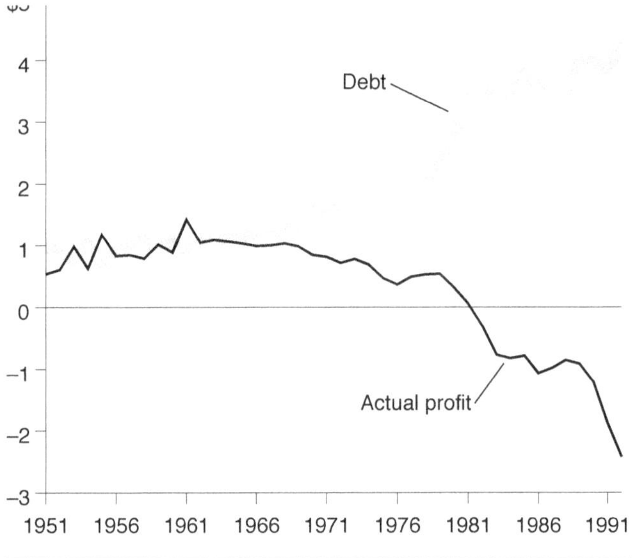

Source: EIR.

ance-sheet derivatives speculation, the figure is fairly estimated to have fallen to the vicinity of 1% or less.

3) Meanwhile, especially since 1987, the rate of daily financial turnover on markets has zoomed; since 1991, the ratio of the curve of rising volume of financial aggregates to rates of per-capita physical-economic output and input, has been indisputably hyperbolically upward.

Those three combined conditions define a rapid convergence upon an absolute functional discontinuity: not merely a financial collapse, but also a potential, literal disintegration of most of the world's monetary and financial institutions.

The only alternative to these calamities would be that governments, particularly the government of the U.S.A., act to put the entire bubbling system into government-supervised financial-bankruptcy reorganization: writing off the claims by fictitious capital, while assuring those continued flows of pensions, withdrawals from modest personal savings, and so on, needed for social, political, and physical-economic stability. Those emergency measures would not be sufficient by themselves, but they are no less indispensable; bankruptcy, "Chapter 11"-style, is the precondition for success of those governmental measures needed to organize an immediate economic recovery.

Under the U.S. Federal Constitution of 1787-89, the means for launching economic recovery are elementary. Within the same 48-hour interval, the President of the U.S.A. declares the Federal Reserve System as a whole to be bankrupt, and places it under the equivalent of "Chapter 11" financial reorganization. On the same day, the Fed is ordered to cease all new issues of Federal Reserve notes; the same day, an emergency bill is sent to Congress, under provisions of Article I, creating several trillions of dollars of U.S. Treasury currency-notes for lending. The loans are issued through a newly created (by act of Congress) National Bank, modelled upon the Washington-Hamilton Bank of the United States. Loans are issued, at between 1% and 2% per annum, in the mode of construction progress-payment tranches, to worthy infrastructure projects operating under authority of emergency legislation, to vendors to those projects, and to other designated high-priority purposes. Success is counted in the number of new productive work-places filled, and in the ration of both the unemployed and the uselessly employed (such as financial-house employees) transferred into productive work-places.

During the same 48 hours the U.S. government is launching those recovery measures at home, the President of the U.S.A. invites the heads of responsible and willing nation-states to appear in Washington, D.C. for emergency sessions establishing both 1) a new international monetary order, replacing the IMF, and 2) guidelines for a new set of bilateral and multilateral tariff and trade agreements; a set of protectionist financial, monetary, and economic agreements reflecting the common vital interests of sovereign nation-states engaged in a general recovery-effort.

One concluding observation is to be added here, before turning to address directly the three questions posed at the outset.

The key to understanding the causes for the imminent disintegration of the present global monetary and financial system—the IMF system—is to recognize the crucial difference between a financial system and a real economy upon which a financial system is superimposed. For that reason, the solution to the problems of economic analysis, which we are next to consider here, depends upon recognizing several considerations which are axiomatic preconditions for competence in economic science. Several among those axiomatic matters are treated in their appropriate place, below; one must be considered at this juncture.

The systems of money, financial accounting, and John Von Neumann's "systems analysis"[26] are each and all *linear* systems. They can represent only those kinds of relations which are themselves approximately of a linear form. Using the language of the undergraduate thermodynamics classroom, they can represent only systems which are either actually entropic, or virtually so.

Contrast, the rise of the human population from the several millions maximum possible for a variety of higher ape: to several hundred millions by the mid-Fourteenth Century, and to more than 5 billions presently. This is the result of willful forms of cultural changes, improvements in demographic characteristics of households and productivity per capita, changes brought about through the discovery of new scientific and related types of principles, a kind of creative-mental behavior which exists only in the member of the human species. This latter set of facts demonstrates, that human behavior is intrinsically not-entropic, neither linear, nor simply "non-linear."[27]

Thus, the monetary-financial system of accounting is a linear system, which cannot map the characteristic events of the not-entropic process which a physical economy represents. The two systems are axiomatically mutually exclusive, with the qualification that a non-entropic system can always represent a linear one, but a linear one can never represent a not-entropic, or even a merely non-linear one. The irony of the matter is, that during the past 500 years of (globally-extended) modern European civilization, the system of agro-industrial economy which dominated the world from the early Eighteenth Century, through the time of President John F. Kennedy's assassination, has been a system based upon the mutual interaction of two axiomatically distinct processes, the financial system and the economic process.

For economic analysis, this difference signifies that all of the real profit (sometimes termed the "macroeconomic profit") of the real economy, the physical economy, is generated through creative (not-entropic) impulses such as technological progress from within the real economy. The financial system as such can generate no such profit; it can merely appropriate wealth from the real economy. This poses the special situation, in which the real economy generates no "macroeconomic profit," or is even operating at a physical-economic loss, in which the financial system appears to be enjoying a high degree of profitability, if but temporarily. This anomalous discrepancy between real and financial profit is sometimes termed "primitive accumulation": the looting of the real economy, and nature itself: a purely parasitical role of the monetary and financial system.

---

26. Von Neumann, op. cit. More descriptive than "systems analysis," is the term which Von Neumann himself employed in introducing his economics, during the late 1930s: *systems of simultaneous linear inequalities*.

27. Too frequently, a streak of scientific illiteracy found even among ostensibly educated professionals, confuses ``not-entropic'' with ``non-linear.'' As noted earlier here, those physical processes, including physical economies, which are not-entropic, can be represented mathematically only in the manner suggested by Cantor's theorem on the enumerability of the density of mathematical discontinuities within an arbitrarily selected interval of action. The advances in technology, as in culture generally, which render one culture superior to another, reflect cumulative, valid discoveries (e.g., mathematical discontinuities in previously established theorem-lattices)--in physical science and in Classical forms of culture--which constitute increases in the number of historically accumulated discontinuities transmitted to an interval of thought-directed practice of today's member of society. Those who blunder into using ``non-linear'' to signify ``not-entropic,'' thus show themselves illiterate respecting the dominant, continuing issue of scientific method throughout the present century: the conflict between Leopold Kronecker, James Clerk Maxwell, and Rayleigh, on the one side, and Carl F. Gauss, Wilhelm Weber, Bernhard Riemann, Karl Weierstrass, and Georg Cantor, on the other.

Until 1963, the two interacting, axiomatically-distinct processes interacted in a kind of symbiosis: Within the industrialized nations, finance, usually, contented itself to taking no more than a share of the "macroeconomic" profit generated by the agro-industrial economic process as a whole. The introduction of the cult of "post-industrial society," together with the degeneration of Bretton Woods into a parasitical form of "floating exchange-rate" monetary system, broke the symbiosis: Finance was transformed from a relatively benign, to a malignant form of financial "cancer."

2. Adam Smith, Sociology, and Newton

During the 1940s and 1950s, since the popularization of the pseudo-science cults of "operations research," "information theory," "econometrics," and "systems analysis," the economics profession has been dominated by charlatans whose abracadabra is expressed in densely-packed mathematical and quasi-mathematical symbols, such as Sigmas, Integral signs, and so on, at the classroom blackboard, or upon the printed page. Some of this twaddle has limited, practical engineering uses; it is like a police-detective's snitch: The detective might use one, with approbation from his superiors; but he should be fired from the force, if he married it. Similarly, the limited, circumscribed usefulness of some of the engineering knick-knacks acknowledged, the prevailing fact of the matter is, that to pretend that that sort of mathematics proves anything of principled importance for economic science, is spewing buncombe.

Why have almost all the economics professionals failed, during the past 30 years, to recognize that current policy-trends were generating a general collapse of the existing monetary and financial systems? Why did all those supposed experts on economic haberdashery fail to recognize, that the Emperor's new suit of clothes left him stark naked? A very large part of the answer to that question, is that, like today's credulous layman, most professionals, too, are devotees of the delusion, that science equals statistics, the delusion that "generally accepted university-classroom" sorts of mathematics are the standard of proof for science.

There are other reasons for this prevailing ignorance of both the professionals and most ordinary citizens; but, as we shall now proceed to demonstrate, those other reasons reflect the same incompetent assumptions which permeate professional ignorance of the problems of generally accepted classroom mathematics. Let the case of Isaac Newton serve as the starting-point for this line of investigation.

The incompetence of Isaac Newton's variety of mathematical physics was exposed as incompetent by the greatest scientific mind of the past three and a half centuries, Gottfried Leibniz.[28] It was seen as an object for contempt by the largest concentration of the world's leaders in science and technology at the beginning of the Nineteenth Century, Gaspard Monge's 1794-1814 Ecole Polytechnique.[29] Newton's method was exposed as scientifically illiterate by the second most brilliant scientific mind of the Nineteenth Century (second to his patron, Carl F. Gauss), Bernhard Riemann.[30] Newton's

---

28. The most widely known among Leibniz's descriptions of the crucial incompetencies within the work of Isaac Newton are from the so-called Leibniz-Clarke correspondence. A convenient reference on this is found in Leory E. Loemker, *Gottfried Wilhelm Leibniz: Philosophical Papers and Letters,* Vol. II (Chicago: University of Chicago Press, 1956), pp. 1095-1169.

29. In the aftermath of Leonardo da Vinci's 1506 flight from Italy, to the patronage of France's Charles d'Amboise on the Loire, France emerged quickly as the European nation-state which, by the early Seventeenth Century, was most advanced in science and technology. France continued to enjoy that superiority over other nations until the post-1814 Bourbon Restoration. The figures of Gaspard Desargues, Pierre Fermat, and Blaise Pascal, and the great *Académie des Sciences* founded and patronized by France's Minister Jean-Baptiste Colbert, typified this during the lifetime of Leibniz. The 1794-1814 version of the Ecole Polytechnique, under the leadership of Gaspard Monge and Adrien M. Legendre, is a high point in this scientific heritage. From 1815 onward, under the pro-Newtonian leadership of the Marquis de LaPlace and Augustin Cauchy, the Ecole Polytechnique and French national academy of science degenerated, with a few exceptions, into what became, predominantly, a swamp of positivism. By approximately 1827, with the establishment of Crelle's Journal (*Journal für reine und angewandte Mathematik*), the Germany of Carl F. Gauss, Alexander von Humboldt, Lejeune Dirichlet, and, later, Bernhard Riemann, assumed a position of world leadership in science, which Germany maintained until the aftermath of World War I. Ridicule of the silly René Descartes and of the sillier Isaac Newton, was standard fare among those world leaders in science occupying the foremost positions, as followers of Gottfried Leibniz, within the Ecole Polytechnique.

30. See the concluding section from Riemann's *Fragmente philosophischen Inhalts,* in *Bernhard Riemann's Gesammelte Mathematische Werke* (New York: Dover Publications, Inc., 1953), pp. 524-525. Note the following excerpts from page 525:
"Das Wort Hypothese hat jetzt eine etwas andere Bedeutung als bei Newton. Man pflegt jetzt unter Hypothese Alles zu den Erscheinungen Hinzugedachte zu verstehen.
"Newton war weit entfernt von dem ungereimten Gedanken, als könne

Newts of a feather: Isaac Newton (left) and Speaker of the U.S. House of Representatives Newt Gingrich. The fact that Gingrich's backers are utterly ignorant about Newton's views on mathematics, does not let them off the hook for supporting the ideological garbage of "free trade."

nority among notable professionals has staked its reputations upon exposing one or more among the additional incompetencies in the Newtonian scheme.[32] Perhaps, the event which the Newtonians found the most embarrassing of all, occurred when the economist John Maynard Keynes was entrusted with examining the contents of the chest of Newton's private papers; Keynes showed that Newton's work had been chiefly kookery in the field of black magic, with virtually nothing of redeemably scientific interest among all of those papers.[33]

Those fallacies in Newton's mathematics which were attacked by Leibniz, by the circles of the Ecole Polytechnique's Gaspard Monge, and by Riemann, are also the key to what makes today's generally accepted classroom "mathematical economics" worse than worthless as a way of representing the way in which economies actually do, or should function.

At this point, we imagine we can see someone in our readership audience raising a finger to interrupt this line of argument. Let us hear his objection. What he has to say might be expressed as the following quotable argument:

> I think I see where you are going with this. Assume, for sake of argument, that your criticisms of Newton and the mathematical economists are correct. How do you answer the objec-

notions of cause-effect were implicitly destroyed by the greatest discovery of scientific principle which has occurred during the Twentieth Century, Max Planck's development of the quantum of action.[31] Otherwise, a mi-

---

die Erklärung der Ersheinungen durch Abstraction gewonnen werden.
"Newton: Et haec de deo; de quo utique ex phaenomenis disserere ad philosophiam experimentalem pertinet. Rationem vero harum Gravitatis propietatum ex phaenomenis nondum potui deducere, et Hypotheses non fingo. Quicquid enim ex Phaenomenis non deducitur, Hypothesis vocanda est.
"Arago, Oeuvres complètes T.3. 505:
"Une fois, une seule fois Laplace s'élança dans la région des conjectures. Sa conception ne fut alors rien moins qu'une cosmogonie.
"Laplace auf Napoleon's Frage, weshalb in seiner Méc[anique] cél[este] der Name Gottes nicht vorkomme: Sire, je n'avais pas besoin de cette hypothèse."
In the same location, Riemann launches his attack against the arbitrariness of the assumption that gravitation must be mathematically equivalent to inertia:
"Die Unterscheidung, welche Newton zwischen Bewegungsgesetzen oder Axiomen und Hypothesen macht, scheint mir nicht haltbar. Das Trägheitsgesetz ist die Hypothese: Wenn ein materieller Punkt allein in der Welt vorhanden wäre und sich im Raum mit einer bestimmten Geschwindigkeit bewegte, so würde er diese Geschwindigkeit beständig behalten."
31. For an historical account of Planck's discovery and the attack upon

Planck by the followers of Ernst Mach, Bertrand Russell, et al., see Caroline Hartman, "A Tragedy of Science: The Life of Max Planck," *21st Century Science & Technology,* Summer 1995.
32. Alfred O'Rahilly, *Electromagnetic Theory, A Critical Examination of Fundamentals* (New York: Dover Publications, Inc., 1938). Originally published as *Electromagnetics,* 1938.
33. See John M. Keynes, "Newton the Man," *Newton Tercentenary Celebration* (Cambridge, U.K.: Cambridge University Press, 1947). Keynes describes Isaac Newton as, "the last of the magicians, the last of the Baylonians and Sumerians ... wholly devoid of scientific value."

tion, that most people who support "free trade" today, have no formal education in mathematics, and would not recognize the differences between Leibniz and Newton? In other words, how does your argument about mathematics apply to the vast majority among those science-illiterates who voted for Newt Gingrich's "Contract with America" in the 1994 elections?

To go directly to the point of the question: The spread of ignorance and superstition is not confined to graduates of today's institutions of higher education. Consider a real-life anecdote, one which should suggest to virtually any reader some relevant evidence already at his or her disposal, addressing the referenced objection.

During 1992, the writer was acquainted with a number of persons who were engaged in studying how to make a living, using modest investable resources, for speculating in futures. That was at a time that "financial derivatives" had begun to capture relatively widespread popular attention, at about the time this speculative frenzy began to assume the sociological characteristics of the Seventeenth-Century tulip bubble. "You see: you can't lose," was the remark that first drew the writer's attention to the kind of impact the derivatives bubble was making within one stratum of the people in his immediate surroundings: very ordinary people, of the specific sort one would classify as "typical small businessmen."

"You can't lose"? The relevant reaction to that, is the time-worn U.S. popular proverb which runs: "Famous last words." The stratum referenced were not uneducated, but were, nonetheless, laymen in the sense implied by the conjectured query we are addressing here. Readers can recognize other expressions of the same social phenomenon in persons much more poorly educated than the subjects of the anecdote just referenced.

In the United States, as elsewhere, it is difficult to convince most members of Wall Street Yuppie generations, that the mere act of obtaining the combination to a neighbor's safe, does not earn one the right to possess the contents of that safe: "I did the work; it's mine!" The real-life persons of the referenced anecdote were not concerned with whether the betting-scheme they were studying contributed anything useful to the economy, or served any other morally significant purpose, excepting the wishful prospect of their own enrich-

ment. Even the notion that their gain would be someone else's loss, was refused by most of those students of this scheme; most believed that "Don't you see: No one loses." "No one loses": the remembered voice of every dupe gulled into joining a "chain-letter" scheme.[34]

Examine the "No one loses" delusion through the eyes of a modern Socrates, and the appropriate response to the objector's proposition emerges. What are the axiomatic qualities of assumption which underlie the controlling delusion of the participant in a "chain-letter" scheme such as the "financial derivatives" racket?[35]

The most conspicuous of the axiomatic assumptions underlying the referenced type of social phenomenon are two: first, the nominalist's metaphysical delusion, that money, by virtue of having the apparent power to command wealth, is wealth; the second, a delusion which Mrs. Joan Robinson has identified as characteristic of all of the professional output of Prof. Milton Friedman, *post hoc ergo propter hoc*.[36] Although Friedman's doctrine is tailored for the opinions of people of whom it is often said, that "their I.Q. is

---

34. Typical cases of this "No one loses" sort of mass-hysteria, in addition to the Seventeenth-Century tulip bubble in the Netherlands, include the Eighteenth-Century "South Sea Island" and "Mississippi" bubbles of John Law's time, and, during the recent half-century, the "Pyramid Club" mass-hysteria of 1949, and compulsive speculator Anthony DeAngelis's 1963-64 "salad-oil bubble." See Norman C. Miller, *The Great Salad Oil Swindle* (Baltimore, Md.: Penguin Books, Inc., 1966).

35. A subsidiary question might be added: Why are present generations of young adults, for example, more susceptible to such delusions than their parents' or grandparents' generations?

36. See Joan Robinson, *Economic Heresies* (New York: Basic Books, Inc., 1971), pp. 86-87; e.g., "…the modern Chicagoans, led by Milton Friedman. A great part of their work consists in historical investigations of the relationship between changes in the supply of money and national income in the United States. The correlations to be explained could be set out in quantity theory terms if the equation were read right-handed.… But the tradition of Chicago consists in reading the equation from left to right. Then the observed relations are interpreted without any hypothesis at all except *post hoc ergo propter hoc*. There is an unearthly, mystical element in Friedman's thought. The mere existence of a stock of money somehow promotes expenditure.…" See, also: Lyndon H. LaRouche, Jr. and David P. Goldman, *The Ugly Truth About Milton Friedman* (New York: New Benjamin Franklin House, 1980). The "dust jacket" of the latter text quotes economist Arthur Laffer: "You want to prove that Milton Friedman is a fascist? It's easy. Quote him." Following Laffer's advice, the publisher cites Friedman's *Studies in the Quantity Theory of Money* (Chicago: University of Chicago Press, 1956): "The object of such controls (on wages, prices, and credit) is the restriction of spending on the part of individuals.… Such a policy, if rigorously enforced, should restrain a rise in the price level. This policy appeared to have been successful in Nazi Germany."

lower than their body-temperature," for just that reason, its advantage for our purposes here, is that it has, correspondingly, few surface features which might distract our attention from the bare axiomatic assumptions which underlie it.

At this point, our response to the objection being considered, assumes the form: Professionals and science illiterates alike accept the putative authority of generally accepted academic economics dogmas. They do so, not because they have learned the academic litanies involved; the dogmas are popular because they were designed to appeal to the kind of ignorant assumptions which are embedded in the present form of popular culture. The widespread acceptance of the two axiomatic assumptions identified immediately above, shows how deep-rooted features of generally accepted popular belief, generate the kinds of suggestibility upon which the economist snakes play, to hypnotize the populist chickens.

It will save time, if we let the completion of our answer to the considered objection flow from continuing the historical account on which we were embarked at the point of that interruption.

The crucial historical fact is, that the popular assumptions on economics matters are identical to the false axiomatic assumptions employed, from the beginning of the Seventeenth Century, to found what became today's generally accepted university-classroom mathematics. All those forms of relatively popular, contemporary university social doctrine which are termed variously empiricist, positivist, or behaviorist, are derived directly from the same axiomatically flawed ideas of mathematics met in the work of Isaac Newton and his followers. All of the trends in public and higher education popularized in the U.S. during the Twentieth Century, all Twentieth-Century innovations in trends in art and mass entertainment, all new trends in notions of mental health, all new trends in teaching and practice of religion, and all generally accepted practice of so-called "news reporting" in mass media, are products of currents in social theory shaped by what English-language tradition usually identifies as "Newtonian" approaches to mathematical physics.

Newton's degenerated parodies of earlier discoveries in mathematics,[37] and forms of social theory coher-

ing with them, were designed in conformity with blind faith in illiterate assumptions respecting the nature of man, nature, and cause-effect. Those assumptions were already somewhat commonplace then, and are venerated in most universities of the world today.

Modern empiricist economics dogma is rooted in an apology for rule of society by a feudal land-owning aristocracy: the so-called Physiocrat dogma of Dr. François Quesnay.[38] Quesnay's central dogma against state interference in feudal aristocrats' whims, *laissez-faire,* was translated into English by the British East India Company lackey, Adam Smith, as "free trade." The only significant difference was, that Smith's doctrine shifted the rule over society from a feudal aristocracy, to the Venetian species of feudalist financier nobility, as typified by the owners of the British East India Company, Barings Bank, and the Bank of England.[39] Lord Palmerston's asset, Karl Marx,[40] defended Adam Smith and "free trade" against the United States of America, but otherwise shifted the future rulership over society from the London financier nobility to a future world-

---

Rouche, Jr., *The Science of Christian Economy* [Washington, D.C.: Schiller Institute, 1991]; see Chapter VII, Note 8, pp. 471-473), that Newton's formulation for gravitation is derived algebraically from the same famous Third Law of astrophysics discovered by Johannes Kepler, and employed by Kepler to define the measurement of that notion of universal gravitation which had been originally and famously discovered by Kepler.

38. François Quesnay, *Tableau Economique* (1758). Court physician, agent of the Venice intelligence service's powerful Abbot Antonio Conti, and founder of the central doctrines common to all empiricist and positivist eonomic dogma, that of Karl Marx and John Von Neumann included.

39. Smith was a lackey of the most powerful figure of mid- to late-Eighteenth-Century London, perhaps the most powerful Englishman of the entire century, William Fitzmaurice Petty, otherwise commonly identified as Lord Shelburne, or the Marquess of Lansdowne. Shelburne, who served as prime minister himself during parts of 1782 and 1783, negotiated the 1783 Treaty of Paris with both the U.S.A. and French representatives. During that same period, Shelburne created the British Foreign Service (in 1782), putting his lackey, Jeremy Bentham, at the head. Later, he bought, on behalf of Barings Bank, the relevant number of members of the Parliament, to ensure the ascension and long tenure of Prime Minister William Pitt the Younger. He was the key oligarch associated with the British East India Company and Barings Bank. From no later than 1763, Shelburne employed Adam Smith, of later *Wealth of Nations* notoriety, as his lackey, assigning Smith to work on a project for destroying the economy of France, and the autonomy and technological progress of the English colonies in North America. Under Shelburne's patronage, lackey Adam Smith visited France and Switzerland, patching together a theory from appropriate scraps of the work of the Physiocrats.

40. See Webster G. Tarpley, et al., "Lord Palmerston's Multicultural Human Zoo," *EIR,* April 15, 1994.

---

37. Take, for example, the fraudulent teaching, that Isaac Newton discovered "universal gravitation." It is readily shown (see, Lyndon H. La-

government, a "dictatorship of the proletariat." Once one knows the rudiments of Quesnay, Smith, Marx, and the Lausanne school's Leon Walras, every essential feature of today's generally accepted university classroom economics, can be attained with no more than a smidgeon of linear mathematics.[41]

On the other so-called "social sciences." What is known as "political science" in today's university curriculum, was invented, like sociology, by the Bourbon Restoration followers of Isaac Newton: notably, the positivists Saint-Simon and Auguste Comte. Emile Durkheim established "sociology" as a certified "discipline" of universities.[42] Ethnology, known in English as Anthropology, had the same Nineteenth-Century French-positivist patronage. Behaviorist psychology, in its several original varieties, was also a Nineteenth-Century concoction of British empiricists and continental positivists. The method of history practiced academically and professionally today, is a creation of the same array of empiricist and positivist ideologues. Even modern legal doctrine and practice, is derived chiefly from irrationalist currents of empiricist and positivist sociology.[43]

And, so on, for the arts and other matters of broad relevance for "mass culture" today.

---

41. Leon Walras (1834-1910), the putative founder of the so-called "Lausanne School" in positivist economics, was the notable predecessor of John Von Neumann in applying systems of simultaneous linear (Newtonian) expressions to the attempted modelling of economic processes. Those functions are assumed to determine the implicit prices and quantities to be assigned to the factors listed under assumed conditions of equilibrium.

42. Emile Durkheim, *Rules of the Sociological Method* (1895).

43. The two leading irrationalist currents within modern philosophy of law are those similar, but distinct varieties, stemming from British empiricist John Locke (1632-1704) and the German neo-Kantian positivist Friedrich Savigny (1779-1861). Contrary to rumor, the U.S. Federal Constitution was referenced to Gottfried Leibniz (life, liberty, and pursuit of happiness), in rejection of Locke's "life, liberty, and property." Locke did shape the Seventeenth-Century colonial law of the Carolinas, and his influence was resurrected by the preamble and body of the insurrectionary constitution of the American Confederacy. Savigny, popularly identified as the putative father of the Romantic school in law, and a key influence in establishing Kantian irrationalism (separation of *Geisteswissenschaft* from *Naturwissenschaft*) in the domain of fine arts, was infamous on two additional counts. During his lifetime, he was notorious as a confederate of the Metternich agent G.W.F. Hegel, in efforts to ruin the attempts of Alexander von Humboldt to establish modern mathematics and modern physical science at Berlin University. During the 1930s, his influence contributed a key part to establishing the foundations of the Nazi law otherwise associated with Carl Schmitt. A strictly Lockean practice of law would establish a form of fascist tyranny more radical than that Germany suffered under the Hitler regime.

The 'Begats' of Empiricism[44]

Modern empiricism, and its appended, generally accepted forms of university-classroom mathematics and social theory, originate with the mathematician, and powerful monk, Paolo Sarpi. This was the Sarpi whose faction seized control of Venice's power in 1582, and used that power to launch the process of the Venetian oligarchy's takeover of England and the Netherlands. Sarpi launched the efforts which led to the establishment of the British monarchy in 1714, and the later foundations of the British Empire, from 1763 onward.

The array of the creatures whom Sarpi employed for this takeover of England's influential institutions, featured such relevant figures as the mathematican Galileo Galilei, Francis Bacon, and the English monarchy of James I.[45] Galileo had a mathematics student, Thomas Hobbes, better known as an intimate of Francis Bacon. Out of these origins, came the relevant, celebrated figures of René Descartes, John Locke, Isaac Newton, David Hume, Charles Montesquieu, and such Eighteenth-Century devotees of Newton (and haters of Leibniz) as Voltaire, Pierre-Louis Maupertuis, Giammaria Ortes, Francesco Algarotti, Leonhard Euler, Joseph Lagrange, the Marquis Laplace, and so on.

Modern science itself had been founded circa A.D. 1440, by Nicolaus of Cusa's *De Docta Ignorantia,* the book which shaped the work of such self-proclaimed followers of Cusa as Luca Pacioli and Leonardo da Vinci. At the beginning of the Seventeenth Century, the most famous acknowledged follower of Cusa, Pacioli, and Leonardo da Vinci, was Johannes Kepler, the founder of the first modern, comprehensive mathematical physics. Followers of Kepler included such famous French mathematicians as Gaspard Desargues, Pierre Fermat, and Blaise Pascal; other followers of the work of Cusa, Leonardo da Vinci, and Kepler included such associates of France's Colbertist *Académie des Sciences* as the Dutchman Christian Huyghens and the German Gottfried Leibniz. The followers of Cusa based the development of modern science upon the pre-established foundations of the Classical Greek work of Plato's Athens Academy and Archimedes.

Cusa's launching of modern science had been com-

---

44. The content of the following sections overlaps material covered earlier in several published locations, notably: Lyndon H. LaRouche, Jr., "'Structures of Sin' Still Rule the Nations," *EIR* April 28, 1995, pp. 46-56

45. Cf. Webster G. Tarpley, "Venice's War Against Western Civilization," *Fidelio,* Summer 1995.

plemented by the use of the Classical Greek tradition for launching deep-going revolutions in the fine arts of poetry, music, tragedy, painting, and architecture, and in related advances in city-building and colonization. This combined scientific and artistic ascent of Fifteenth-Century Europe out of the Fourteenth-Century "New Dark Age," is the *Renaissance.*

The opponents of Cusa's, Leonardo's, Kepler's, and Leibniz's current of modern science, based themselves upon the deductive and metaphysical methods of Plato's adversary Aristotle. Venice's (and Padua's) Aristotelean efforts to eradicate modern science, were superseded by Paolo Sarpi's rise to the leading position of power in Venice's foreign policy. Sarpi's neo-Aristotelean method, which harked back in part to nominalists such as William of Ockham, became known variously as *empiricism,* or the *Enlightenment.*

It is useful and fair to say, that all of the past five centuries of the internal history of extended European civilization, has been a continuing war of the Venice-launched *Enlightenment* against the *Renaissance.* The two represent mutually exclusive conceptions of the nature of man, and of the universe; consequently, these axiomatic differences subsume mutually exclusive notions of the nature of cause-effect relations within society, and in man's practical (e.g., physical-economic) interaction with the universe. That conflict, between the ideas of the Renaissance and the contrary, empiricist ideas of the reactionary Enlightenment, has shaped the internal and global history of extended modern European civilization throughout the past five centuries.

This conflict in ideas has an easily recognized practical basis.

Prior to the Fifteenth-Century Renaissance in western Europe, in all cultures, throughout all prior existence, over 95% of humanity had lived in the depressed condition of virtual human cattle, as serfs, slaves, or worse. The typical structure of ancient and medieval society, throughout the planet, had been the picture of society offered by the first part of Aeschylus' famous tragedy, *Prometheus*[46]: at the top of society, a collection of ``quasi-immortal'' oligarchical families, the real-life guise of the Greek gods of Olympus; immediately below them, their lackeys, who administered the

affairs of mankind on orders from Olympus; below that, the 95% subject to the capricious whims of the oligarchs.

The influence of the A.D. 1439-40 sessions of the Council of Florence, and the echoing effects of Louis XI's accession to the throne of France in A.D. 1461, changed the human condition radically. With the transformation of a reconstructed France into the first modern nation-state, under Louis XI, the order of human affairs was revolutionized, with the effects of that revolution radiating throughout this planet to the present day. The policy of fostering a humanist form of secondary education for orphans and for boys from families of the poor, broke the barrier which had earlier confined more than 90% of humanity permanently to a cattle-like status under oligarchical domination. The building of the modern form of sovereign nation-state republic, sometimes called a "commonwealth," on this new social basis, was, and is the modern nation-state.

That new institution, the modern nation-state, has revolutionized the rate of growth of potential population-density, of productive powers of labor, and demographic characteristics of family households.[47] Taking into account all of the just complaints to be placed at the door of the nations of modern Europe and North America, any elimination of the institution of the sovereign nation-state would unleash a global genocide beyond any criminality earlier wreaked upon humanity in known history up to this point.

These new, Renaissance institutions, the policies of the Council of Florence and the modern nation-state, came immediately into mortal conflict with two oligarchical forces: the landed feudal aristocracy, and the financial oligarchy led by, and typified by, the Venice nobility. The powerful new forces sent into motion by the Renaissance came near to crushing Venice at the beginning of the Sixteenth Century; Venice's successful use of corruption to set its powerful enemies against one another's throats, breaking up the anti-Venice League of Cambrai, enabled Venice to survive, and recover much of its strength, through continuing such "balance of power" diplomacy.[48] Nonetheless, during the follow-

---

46. *Prometheus Bound,* in *Aeschylus,* Herbert Weir Smyth, trans., Vol. II (Cambridge, Mass.: [Loeb Classical Library] Harvard University Press, 1922); pp. 211-315.

47. See Lyndon H. LaRouche, Jr., "What Is God, that Man Is in His Image?" *Fidelio,* Spring 1995: graphs and chart on population and demographics, pp. 25-26.

48. Tarpley, "Venice's War," op. cit., passim.

ing three centuries, all feudalist efforts to destroy the modern nation-state failed. The Holy Alliance, the last major expression of feudal-aristocratic imperial power, disintegrated in 1848-49, and its relics were virtually obliterated[49] during the course of World War I. The financier oligarchy has been a more durable proposition; Sarpi is key to understanding why.

The root of the nation-states' inevitable defeat of the feudal aristocracy's imperial institutions, is found in effects of the nation-state's tendencies toward universal humanist education for the youth from families of the poor. The tendencies toward future universal education, combined with emphasis upon technological improvements in the productive powers of labor, revolutionized economy and warfare. Among similar effects, this educational tendency prompted a qualitative increase in the society's potential, per capita, for generating and assimilating the benefits of scientific and technological progress. The fostering of advances in technology and productive powers of labor, translate into increase in the firepower and mobility of military forces. Against determined modern nation-states, the imperial obsessions of the old feudal land-owning aristocracies were doomed to ultimate defeat.

Sarpi and his faction committed themselves to establishing a global maritime and financier power within the Protestant regions of northern Europe, selecting the Netherlands and England as the new centers of global maritime power, in which to build up such clones of the Venice oligarchical system. Instead of seeking to destroy the nation-state, they sought to dominate it from within, by a combination of control over the finances of the nation-state, and through balance-of-power games pitting one nation-state against the other. In this way, the modern nation-state became, predominantly, a form of "mixed economy" which combined the nation-state's original and organic impulse for agro-industrial investment in technological progress, with the superimposition of a financier oligarchy, controlling the financial and monetary institutions of the nation-state, on top.

Sarpi's "new Venetians" of Paris, London, and the Netherlands, put three conditions upon their willingness to tolerate the institutions of the modern sovereign nation-state. The first condition: The Venetian-style, London-centered financier oligarchy must dominate the world's financial markets and the central banking institutions of the nations. The second condition: The nation-state itself would be tolerated, but not the "Renaissance" quality of intellect and spirit which had brought the new form of European society into being at the Council of Florence and under France's Louis XI. The third condition: The relations among nation-states must be regulated by the same "divide and rule" ("balance of power") practices which Venice itself had employed to set its enemies within the League of Cambrai at one another's throats.

Our topic here, is the second of those three conditions: the methods which these Venetians and their neo-Venetian British clones employed, to adopt the babies, the nation-states as such, after sterilizing both those babies and their parents, ridding the population of the intellectually and morally fertile influences of the Renaissance. The topic here is those methods of cultural warfare, psychological and philosophical warfare, which empiricism has used to enslave the minds of those over whom it rules. Once the Sarpi-Galileo-Hobbes-Descartes-Newton development of a perverted form of mathematics is understood, and the way in which today's generally accepted university-classroom social theory was derived from that empiricist mathematics, the mechanisms which control the minds of most U.S.A. citizens today, are immediately recognizable. That is the key to the persistence of the presently ongoing economic debacle.

That said, turn to consider the manner in which the Europe-wide salons created by Sarpi's most important successor, Abbot Antonio Conti,[50] controlled the des-

___

49. Or, assimilated, with or without their aristocratic titles, into the ranks of the Anglo-Dutch international financier nobility, as the English and Scottish feudal aristocracy had been earlier.

50. Antonio Conti, pen-name "Schinella," the most important oligarchical figure of Eighteenth-Century Europe, but today among the least known to history students. Born as a member of the Venice nobility, in Padua, 1677, a descendant of the Nani clan, on his mother's side, and of Sperone Speroni, himself an influential student of the founder of the Padua school of Aristotle, Pietro Pompanazzi. In 1699, young Conti entered the Venice religious order *Oratorio pardi della Fava,* and was ordained as a priest, but abandoned those vows in 1708. He became a specialist in French culture, including the study of modern science of that time from the standpoint of René Descartes, remaining a secular priest with the title of "abbot." During this time-frame, Conti assumed a leading role in the formation of a network of Europe-wide Venice intelligence-service salons, *conversazione filosofica e felice.* (See Piero de Negro, *Giammaria Ortes: un "filosofico" veneziano del Settecento* Cini Foundation study of 1990 [Florence, Italy: L.S. Olschki, 1993], pp. 125-182.) The principal target of his work was organizing a continent-wide

tiny of every nation of Europe over the course of the Eighteenth Century. From approximately 1582 through the death of Conti in 1749, Venice's agents Sarpi and Conti are the two most significant figures of the European Enlightenment, the two cabalists who virtually created the mythical nation of Britain from mud. We touch only the most relevant highlights of the Conti salon's "begats" here.[51]

Members of Conti's Newton cult included such notables as Charles Montesquieu (*Spirit of the Law*, 1750) and Voltaire. Also an agent of Conti's salon, was the Dr. François Quesnay who produced the dogma of "free trade" (*laissez-faire*). The most important figures of the salon, after Conti himself, were, first, the Venetian Camaldolesian monk Giammaria Ortes, and second, the Camaldolesian abbot, and teacher of Ortes and Francesco Algarotti, Pisa's Guido Grandi. One of the key European figures controlled by the Conti Salon was Prussia's Frederick II, the so-called "Frederick the Great." A nest of Conti's Leibniz-hating Newton-cult figures controlled Frederick II's Berlin Academy of Science: the hoaxster Pierre-Louis Maupertuis, his accomplice in the hoax, Leonhard Euler, "pretty boy" Francesco Algarotti, who set the pace for the degenerate aesthetical dogmas of Immanuel Kant's 1790 *Critique of Judgment,* and Pierre-Louis Lagrange.[52] Throughout all Europe, there was no center of scientific thought in which Isaac Newton enjoyed a favorable reputation, which was not controlled by the agents of Conti's Venetian networks of salons.

The same network of Venetian salons also deployed, against the French monarchy, the "sting agents" Giacomo Casanova and, later, Alessandro Cagliostro.

The key figure to study, to expose the manner in which these Venetians around Sarpi and Conti's salon pasted together their perverted brand of mathematics and their social theory, is Giammaria Ortes (1713-90): the "father of Malthusianism,"[53] and also the principal coordinator of the Europe-wide efforts leading to the syncretic concoction known as the British East India Company's Haileybury school of economics: Adam Smith, Jeremy Bentham, Thomas Malthus, David Ricardo, James Mill, John Stuart Mill, et al.

The social dogma which Ortes et al. concoct, to form the basis for what became Adam Smith's "free trade" hokum, is traced directly from Galileo's mathematics pupil Thomas Hobbes, by way of John Locke, et al. The clearest insight into the British empiricist's understanding of this dogma, is a 1725 book by a Dutch-born rapscallion, of the name of Bernard Mandeville, *The Fable of the Bees: Private Vices, Public Benefits.* Mandeville gives the show away, by pointing out that the British empiricist's notion of "freedom" rests on the remarkable presumption, that it is immoral, even outrightly evil deeds by individual persons, which produce all of society's ultimate good.

A recent weekend (July 15-16, 1995) edition of the London *Financial Times,* illustrates the point, employing author Lyall Watson's stomach-wrenching efforts at making the point with attempts at typically Oxbridge "British understatement." The article, featured on page 1 of the weekend section, is entitled "The Case for Cannibalism," a slug which leers out from under a six-column photograph image of a primitive Asmat cannibal tribesman. The caption reads: "The Asmat have turned population dynamics into an intricate and strangely beautiful game: they eat each other, happily." A few passages from that piece are quotable, to assure the reader that Watson (and the *Financial Times*) are quite serious about this promotion of cannibalism, and

---

effort, creating the cult of Isaac Newton as a vehicle for seeking to eliminate the name and influence of Gottfried Leibniz. He was personally deployed to Hanover for this purpose, following up efforts by his agent Ludovico Antonio Muratori. His letters from London and notebooks of that same period identify his close association with Isaac Newton, Edmond Halley, Samuel Clarke (of the Leibniz-Clarke Correspondence), Willem-Jacob Gravesande, Abraham deMoivre, and James Stirling. (See Antonio Conti, *Scritti filosofici* [Naples: F. Rossi, 1972] and Mauro di Lisa, *"Chi mi sa dir s'io fingo, Newtonianismo e scetticismo in Giammaria Ortes,"* *Giornale critico della filosofia italiana,* LXVII [1988], pp. 221-233.) In London, Conti established himself as a Kensington Whig, the political party of the followers of William of Orange, Marlborough, et al.

51. For more background, see Lyndon H. LaRouche, Jr., "How Bertrand Russell Became an Evil Man," *Fidelio,* Fall 1994, and Webster G. Tarpley, "Venice's War," op. cit.

52. Some German patriots sneaked Ephraim Lessing, the friend of Moses Mendelssohn, into the Academy, behind Frederick's back, so to speak; Frederick acted to ensure that Moses Mendelssohn was not appointed, too.

53. Giammaria Ortes, *Reflessioni sulla popolazione delle nazioni per rapporto all'economia nazionale* (Venice: 1790). This book, published soon after in an English edition, was the basis which Jeremy Bentham's Rev. Thomas Malthus plagiarized in producing his *An Essay on Population* (1790) (New York: E.P. Dutton and Co., 1960). The notion of "carrying capacity," which the Club of Rome inserted into the population-policy discussions of the 1980s, is taken directly from Ortes's *Reflessioni,* not Malthus. For more on Ortes, see Lyndon H. LaRouche, Jr., "How Bertrand Russell Became an Evil Man," loc. cit., passim.

The British oligarchical mind at work, in the London Financial Times of July 15-16, 1995: "Some of my best friends are cannibals. . . . "

that we might prepare the reader for an insight into the minds of not only the perverse Mandeville, but Hobbes, Locke, and Ortes, too.

Watson begins: "Some of my best friends are cannibals. They live on the Casuarina Coast, the delta area of Irian in Indonesian New Guinea.... There are about 20,000 of them and they call themselves the Asmat, which means 'the human beings.' All outsiders are known very simply as Manowe—'the edible ones.'" Near the close of the article, on the jump page, Watson waxes British-philosophical as he gets down to empiricist business: "The fact that humans are, on occasion, both aggressive and violent presents the Asmat with no problem and requires no heart-searching or remorse. They have stereotyped and ritualised such tendencies, allowing them full and satisfying play in headhunting, *while at the same time resolving a pressing environmental problem* [emphasis added].... There is hope in this, but only if we follow the Asmat example and learn how to bend in favour of that which best allows equilibrium to be established."

That is exactly what Mandeville means by "private vices, public benefits," and what Adam Smith defines as individual morality in his 1759 *The Theory of the Moral Sentiments.* That is the same construction which François Quesnay employs in arguing that society must benefit from non-interference with the capricious whims of feudal aristocratic serf-owners—*laissez-faire*—and the argument which Adam Smith copies from Quesnay in

presenting his case for "free trade" in the 1776 *Wealth of Nations.* That is way in which Thomas Hobbes argues in his *Leviathan*; that is the morality of John Locke, and Jean-Jacques Rousseau. That is, as the item from the *Financial Times* merely reflects this, the typical, present-day British-empiricist mind-set; that is the mind-set expressed by the attitude of British diplomats and U.N.O. officials in explaining why Bosnians must submit to Chetnik conquest by means of rape and genocide, for the greater good of a reunited Yugoslavia under control of London's and Milosevic's Chetnik assets.

To understand Hobbes's, Locke's, Mandeville's, Adam Smith's, and Lyall Watson's curious advocacy of individual evil, examine the empiricist axiom we have just described here from the standpoint of the relevant mathematical physics.

Think of the mechanistic model of a Cambridge University gas system, as fancied by Lords Kelvin or Rayleigh, for example: a Newtonian gas system. Construct the image. See the millions of tiny balls roving about in what is otherwise a confined vacuum. Remember that beach-side concession, where, for a brief, but idyllic moment, one might rent the use of an electric-powered "bump-'em" car, ramming other such "bump-'em" cars, and being rammed in turn? So, the tiny gas-particles interact percussively, and, in a more sophisticated version, by radiating upon one another.

Now imagine that each of these tiny balls is motivated by either an assortment of the Seven Deadly Sins, or, perhaps, some motives of a nastier type. In addition to percussive interactions so generated, they also radiate sinful and even evil impulses upon one another. Now, imagine that a net social good comes out of all of this percussive and radiant wickedness. Imagine that this occurs in the fashion Rayleigh's gas would acquire the general attribute of pressure and temperature, through some mechanism analogous to the kind of kinematic equilibrium popular with Galileo, Hobbes, Newton, et al. There you have the intellectual model which forms the axiomatic basis in method for all of the principal theses on social theory in general, and economics in particular, by Hobbes, Locke, Mandeville,

Giammaria Ortes, Adam Smith, Jeremy Bentham, John Stuart Mill, and John Von Neumann.

The hey-day for constructing such social-theory concoctions was the Enlightenment's Eighteenth Century. The central figure in this enterprise was the Conti salon's Ortes; this was understood by Ortes to be the effort to show that all social processes could be reduced to the terms of a mechanistic model, using Newton's algebraic designs as a model. After Ortes's recipe had been assimilated by the British and the continental Newtonians, the empiricists and continental positivists have been virtually mass-producing new departments of social theory, from the second half of the Eighteenth Century, to the present day. It is all essentially gobble-dygook, but the suckers call it "science," or simply "professionalism," nonetheless.

3. How the Control Works

Mother opens the kitchen door, exclaiming, "Junior! You have your hand in the cookie-jar again!"

The boy recovers quickly, and retorts with what might pass for injured innocence: "What cookie-jar?"

Not all charlatans choose to be conscious of the fact that they are practicing fraud.

The poet, dramatist, and historian Friedrich Schiller named one of the important categories of such charlatans. In German, the term is *Brotgelehrten*: In English, it translates as the professional who passed his time in higher education studying to learn how to get a better-paying job after graduation. It is the end-product produced by the student who challenges the teacher: "Teacher, is this going to come up on the examination?" meaning that the student considers it immoral for the teacher to raise any topic for which the pupil is not going to be financially rewarded, sooner or later. In the present writer's long experience, most U.S. professionals—among others—are *Brotgelehrten,* whether or not they speak German.

Any honest scientist works much harder, and with greater rigor than any member of the tribes of the *Brotgelehrten*; he is motivated by the sheer joy of scientific discovery, just as any really good professional musician is similarly driven. He or she is motivated by the consideration, that when doing genuinely creative, rigorous work, his or her mind is in a more ennobled state, a more joyful one, than would be possible were he or she

not so engaged for a large portion of each day, each week. Put aside all the silly litany about "desire for gain, and fear of losses" in the cant of the empiricist economists and sociologists. The essential motive for doing good, is that it is fun: much more fun to be that kind of person, than any other.

The importance of having fun, in that way, is better cognized if one reflects on the brevity of that historical instant we know as the expected life-span of the mortal individual person. Once one grasps that one's foremost self-interest lies in acquisition of those things which one may, assuredly, carry into the grave, the things which are not objects of sensory pleasure or pain, then fun is living in the way which cheats death, the things which leave the world a better place after one has left it, than one found it, a mere historical instant earlier.

Once one has learned the joy of having fun, there are certain questions which come frequently to one's mind, questions which any of the dismal *Brotgelehrten* would probably never think to ask. The *Brotgelehrten* locate self-interest in that which they imagine themselves to get out of the mere historical instant of their mortal existence; people who have fun, worry about what they are putting into that instant. The *Brotgelehrten* are therefore much less intelligent, and also less happy, than the people who have fun.

The sobersided pragmatist, with his eye fixed on what he considers his main chance, will argue in defense of Newton, and so on, "Buddy, this is the way the world is, and if you wish to get ahead, learn to accept the way things work, the way the world is." That miserable sobersides would never think to ask, what kind of mathematics exists outside Newtonianism? He would never think about those facts from the known span of human existence which show us that all empiricist sociology, and economic dogma is flatly absurd from the start.

Thus, the facts we are about to reference will probably appeal only to either those who simply enjoy having fun, or who prefer not to have the world plunged into the kind of New Dark Age in which the population of this planet collapses, very rapidly, through famine, epidemic disease, and perhaps cannibalistic qualities of homicide, from over 5 billions persons today, to less than half a billion 20 to 40 years from now.

That *Brotgelehrten* type, whether he or she has graduated from institutions of higher learning, or is an illiterate, is the bearer of that quality which the empiricist tradition values most highly in its victims. This is what the empiricist tradition has worked to ensure remains the standard of popular culture.

For the citizen who prefers fun, there are two questions which ought to be considered of the utmost importance.

The first involves the factual evidence showing the true nature of the human individual: that, as Moses' first chapter of *Genesis* insists, the created universe is *good,* and the individual person is born not only intrinsically good, but the noblest creature of creation. As this writer has spent most of his adult life insisting that, were man merely an animal, subject to the rules of animal ecology, the human species could never have exceeded a living population of several millions individuals at any time past, under the late Cenozoic conditions prevailing on this planet during the recent 2 millions years. Man, unlike any beast, has the creative-mental capacity to effect valid discoveries of scientific principle, through which to transform man's relations with the universe, and thus to increase the potential population-density of the human species, while improving the demographic characteristics of the family household.

The second, is the question: Since human existence depends upon an unending succession of revolutionary discoveries of principle in natural science, and otherwise, what is the nature of human knowledge? Since mathematical formalism represents knowledge in terms of the kinds of deductive consistency we associate with deductive theorem-lattices, how can we represent the *progress (change)* of knowledge which overturns an existing such theorem-lattice? The fun-loving person who embarks on a rigorous and sustained study of that question, will end up as a follower of Plato, of Nicolaus of Cusa, Leonardo da Vinci, Kepler, Leibniz, Gauss, and Riemann.

There are two conceptions to be mastered. First, the notion of *ideas,* as defined by Plato, which this writer addressed in the Spring 1995 edition of *Fidelio.*[54] Second, the understanding that mathematics remains a useful tool only as long as we introduce the principles of physical science to mathematics from the outside, principles which occur to us in the form of scientific *ideas,* as Plato understood the notion of ideas, and as

Aristotle, Pietro Pomponazzi, Paolo Sarpi, and Isaac Newton did not: as this writer has repeatedly addressed that issue.[55] Once those conceptions are grasped, and implications of those ideas are understood, that person is freed from victimization by that corruption recognized as "popular culture," and will therefore be free from the confidence-game called empiricism.

The crucial thing to be understood, is that the prevailing popular culture is not a "natural" phenomenon, but a synthetic culture, created and shaped by those powerful, presently London-centered international oligarchical forces which have long sought to contain and control the institution of the modern nation-state, and are now committed to seeking to destroy it. Once it is also recognized, what is the significance of the demonstrable frauds permeating Newton's work, and the related frauds permeating taught economics-teaching and social-theory dogma generally, the citizen is no longer gripped by the compulsion to believe that "the cookie jar to which mother refers does not exist."

---

55. See Lyndon H. LaRouche, Jr., "The Fraud of Algebraic Causality," *Fidelio,* Winter 1994.

Lyndon LaRouche's university textbook on national economic policy, which also serves as a manual for government officials and advisors to governments.

---

54. Loc. cit.